Layers of Understanding

Setting Standards for Architectural Paint Research

Proceedings of a seminar held on 28 April 2000

Layers of Understanding

Setting Standards for Architectural Paint Research

Proceedings of a seminar held on 28 April 2000

DONHEAD

© 2002 English Heritage (text)

© Illustrations and photographs: copyright of the authors, unless specified

Simultaneously published in the United Kingdom and Massachusetts, USA by Donhead

All rights reserved. No part of this publication may be reproduced, stored in a retrieval system or transmitted in any form or by any means, electronic, mechanical photocopying, recording or otherwise, without the prior written permission of the copyright owner and publisher.

Published by
Donhead Publishing Ltd
Lower Coombe
Donhead St Mary
Shaftesbury
Dorset SP7 9LY
Tel. 01747 828422
www.donhead.com

ISBN 1 873394 58 6

British Library Cataloguing in Publication Data

> Layers of Understanding
> 1. Paint - Congresses 2. Historic Buildings - Conservation and restoration
> I. Hughes, Helen II. English Heritage
> 729.4'072
> ISBN 1873394586

Library of Congress Cataloging in Publication Data
A Catalog record for this book has been requested

Printed by Alden Press, Oxford

Contents

Acknowledgements	vii
Author Biographies	ix
Foreword by Helen Hughes, Senior Architectural Paint Researcher, English Heritage	xiii

Session 1

1	**Introduction: Architectural Paint Research in a Wider Context** Kate Clark, Head of Historic Environmental Management, English Heritage	3
2	**Historic Overview** Ian Bristow, Architect and Specialist Consultant in the Redecoration of Historic Interiors	9
3	**The Problems Facing the Development of Architectural Paint Research** Helen Hughes	13

Session 2

4	**Some Tips on Commissioning Architectural Paint Research** Patrick Baty, Specialist Consultant on Architectural Paint and Colour	21
5	**Architectural Paint Research in Practice** Ian Jardin, Project Director, Major Projects Department, English Heritage	27
6	**Architectural Paint Research: The Dutch Experience and Perspective** Angelique Friedrichs, Course Director, Decorative Historic Interiors, Stichting Restauratie Atelier Limburg, Maastricht	31

Session 3

7	**Statutory Requirements: Listed Building Requirements and PPG 15** James Edgar, Historic Buildings Inspector, English Heritage	37
8	**Formulating Procedures for Architectural Paint Research** Tina Sitwell, Advisor on the Conservation of Painted Surfaces, The National Trust	41

Session 4

9 Proposed Guidelines for Commissioning Architectural Paint Research   47
Helen Hughes

10 Discussion Sessions   51
chaired by Ian Bristow, Kate Clark and Helen Hughes

Proposed guidelines for commissioning architectural paint research
Reclamation of obliterated finishes
Wallpapers
Reversibility
Paint stripping
Substrates
Funding and programming
Use of black and white photographs
Scrapes versus samples and mounted cross-sections
Training
Programming and risk management
Conservation policies
Samples sent through the post

11 Conclusion   63
Kate Clark

Appendices

Appendix I: Architectural Paint Research Chart and Categorization System   67
Helen Hughes

Appendix II: Paint Strippers: The Naked Truth   73
Cathy Proudlove, Head of Conservation, Norwich Castle Museum

Bibliography   75

Index   77

Acknowledgements

The seminar was held at the Scientific Studies Lecture Theatre in Savile Row on the 28 April 2000 by English Heritage. Thanks for the administration of what was a very successful event should be extended to Amanda Holgate and Maria Nyberg-Coles. Colin Powel was responsible for the management of the technicalities within the lecture theatre, ensuring that the day ran both smoothly and audibly. Margaret Woods provided enthusiastic support for the publication of the seminar proceedings as well as invaluable comments on preliminary drafts. The careful preparation of this document and picture research was carried out by Louise Henderson.

Author Biographies

Patrick Baty
Papers and Paints Ltd

Patrick Baty is an ex Regular Army Officer and since 1980 has been running a small specialist family paint business in London. Inspired by an early talk given by Ian Bristow, he began his research into the architectural use of the paint and colour in the eighteenth and nineteenth centuries and completed a research degree on the 'Methods and Materials of the Housepainter 1600–1850'. Patrick has published a number of articles in *Country Life*, and other publications including *Perspective on Architecture* and the *Journal of Architectural Conservation*, as well as contributing to, and revising, several books on colour and decoration. He lectures often on the general subject of paint and colour of the period to diverse audiences. He is a frequent lecturer on postgraduate courses at several universities to architects and conservation officers, both in the UK, along the East Coast of the United States, and at a number of international symposia in Europe.

Patrick acts as a consultant on paint and colour for English Heritage, The National Trust, Historic Royal Palaces and many private and institutional clients. He has carried out the paint analysis at Uppark, the Painted Room at Spencer House, The National Trust for Scotland headquarters in Charlotte Square and the Privy Garden at Hampton Court.

Patrick is a member of the Executive Committee of the Georgian Group and a founding member of the Traditional Paint Forum.

Ian Bristow, DPhil FSA ARIBA

Ian Bristow is an architect who has specialized in the conservation of historic buildings. From 1975 he held a three-year fellowship at the University of York to undertake research into the use of colour in British Interiors. In 1996 he published *Architectural Colour in British Interiors 1615–1840* and its companion technical volume *Interior House-Painting Colours and Technology 1615–1840*. He is in private practice, giving specialized advice on the redecoration of historic buildings and their interiors. Ian Bristow is a member of the Historic Built Environment Advisory Committee of English Heritage, and Chairman of its Places of Worship Panel. He is also President of the Traditional Paint Forum, Chairman of the Association for Studies in the Conservation of Historic Buildings and a member of the Westminster Abbey Fabric Commission.

Kate Clark
Head of Historic Environmental Management,
English Heritage

Kate Clark is an archaeologist specializing in building and landscapes of the industrial period. She lectured in industrial archaeology at the Ironbridge Institute and was Monuments Manager for the Ironbridge Gorge Trust. She worked as Conservation Officer for the Council of British Archaeology and first joined English Heritage as an Inspector of Ancient Monuments, then headed the Historic Analysis and Research Team. Kate Clark is now head of Historic Environmental Management and has provided training on the Conservation Plan process to a wide range of heritage groups. She is the author of *Informed Conservation* and co-author of *The Landscape of Industry: Patterns of Change in the Ironbridge Gorge*.

James Edgar
English Heritage

James Edgar is an Inspector of Historic Buildings, working for English Heritage since 1986. Before that date he was with the Greater London Council's Historic Buildings Division. Qualifications and experience in a number of disciplines enable him to deal with some historic areas and parks and gardens work in addition to 'pure' historic buildings tasks. For many years he was employed in London, with responsibility for casework in the City of Westminster. Cases on many a public institution, particularly the galleries, museums and learned societies as well as the wonderful gentlemen's clubs and private houses in Mayfair, Marylebone, St James's and Soho, enabled him to have a hand in many proposals involving alterations to important interiors. For the last few years he has been working in the Midland Region of English Heritage.

Angelique Friedrichs
Course Director, Decorative Historic Interiors
Stichting Restauratie Atelier, Maastricht

Angelique Friedrich gained her MA in Art History at the University of Amsterdam on 'The ethical considerations concerning the conservation of stone sculpture, the scientific examination of art objects and the social status of the artist during Quattrocento in Italy'.

Since September 1998 Angelique has been the Course Director of the Conservation Course on Decorative Historic Interiors, part of the training programme of Paintings and Painted Objects, Stichting Restauratie Atelier Limburg, Maastricht, Netherlands, as well as the programme co-ordinator of an international project entitled 'Architectural Heritage, Don't Forget the Historic Interior' in co-operation with the Conservation Scholl in Antwerp.

Helen Hughes
Senior Architectural Paint Researcher
English Heritage

Helen obtained a degree in the History of Art and Architecture at University College London before training as an easel painting conservator at Gateshead Technical College. She has worked with English Heritage in the Architectural Paint Research Unit since 1985 and has obtained UKIC accreditation as an Architectural Paint Researcher.

The Architectural Paint Research Unit is now located within the Building Conservation and Research Team (BCRT) of English Heritage and continues to offer advice on a wide range of projects. One of Helen's recent major projects was supervizing the conservation and redecoration of the seventeenth-century interiors of the Little Castle, Bolsover. The Unit is currently involved in the publication of a volume for the BCRT's Research Transactions series detailing her work at the Little Castle, as well as producing the proceedings of two recent conferences and a standards document for the profession. The Unit provides training to assistants and intern students and houses an extensive database and archive of research carried out on behalf of English Heritage over the last twenty years.

Ian Jardin
Project Director, Major Projects Department,
English Heritage

Ian Jardin has worked for English Heritage almost since its inception. For much of that time as a manager of conservation casework and as Secretary of the Historic Buildings Advisory Committee, he has seen conservation problems and opportunities in almost all their forms. He has completed the Architectural Association Building Conservation course directed by Ian Bristow – which not least enhanced his appreciation of the role of paint research. Ian Jardin has been a Project Director in English Heritage's Major Project Department since its creation in 1995. In that time he has directed several major projects entailing historic interiors, including the rescue of Grade I Danson House, the refurbishment and opening of the 1930s Courtauld House at Eltham Palace and the installation of the Wernher Fine Art Collection within Grade I Ranger's House, Blackheath.

Cathy Proudlove
Head of Conservation, Norwich Castle Museum

Cathy Proudlove trained in conservation of oil paintings at the Courtauld Institute. In the 1970s she worked for the South Eastern Museums Service, followed by three years as conservator at the North Carolina Museum of Art, USA. Since returning to the UK she has worked for Norfolk Museums and Archaeology Service specializing in conservation of painted surfaces, becoming head of department in 1990. Working in East Anglia has generated a deep concern for the preservation of the region's incomparable medieval to eighteenth-century heritage, whether in situ or in a museums context. This inspired an exhibition in 1997, 'True Colour', which highlighted the vulnerability of original painted surfaces in buildings. Her other professional interests include the mutual conservation of collections and historic buildings and preventive conservation of collections. She was a founder member and later, co-ordinator, of the Care of Collections Forum.

Tina Sitwell
Advisor on the Conservation of Painted Surfaces,
The National Trust

Tina Sitwell received a degree in the Conservation of Wall Paintings from the Winterthur Museum/ University of Delaware. Subsequently she was awarded a Smithsonian Fellowship for a postgraduate internship at the Tate Gallery. Tina Sitwell joined The National Trust in 1990 as an Assistant Advisor on Painting Conservation and in 1995 was given responsibility for the Conservation of Painted Surfaces, which includes historic surfaces.

Tina is a member of the Traditional Paint Forum and has been involved in giving lectures at events organised by the Forum since its foundation. She is also a committee member of the recently created Historic Interiors section of the United Kingdom Institute for Conservation of Historic and Artistic Works (UKIC).

Foreword

The one day seminar entitled *Layers of Understanding – Setting Standards for Architectural Paint Research* was convened by English Heritage in consultation with Ian Bristow, to address growing concerns about the variable quality of architectural paint research currently being carried out. Architectural paint research is now recognized as an important discipline in the analysis of buildings. The requirements to assess and understand historic buildings as a basis for making conservation decisions is widely advocated in the United Kingdom. This approach is set out in *Planning Policy Guidance Note 15: Planning and the Historic Environment* (PPG 15) and various English Heritage advisory notes and literature. An awareness of the value of good architectural paint research has fuelled a demand that cannot be met by the small number of experienced researchers currently working in the United Kingdom.

The seminar proved to be an important event in defining the state of architectural paint research at the moment and identifying a wide range of problems and concerns. It was extremely well attended with delegates from Eire, Sweden, Norway, The Netherlands and the USA, emphasizing the widespread interest in the subject. The occasion brought together practitioners and commissioning clients and generated a lively discussion of problems hampering the development of the discipline.

One of the specific aims of the seminar was to discuss the proposed set of standards and guidelines for architectural paint research which could be adopted by clients and consultants alike. All delegates were provided in advance with a copy of the draft English Heritage guidance leaflet on suggested standards for commissioning architectural paint research which had been produced in collaboration with consultants working in the field. Delegates were invited to comment on the contents during the afternoon session of the seminar. The one-day event therefore offered a unique opportunity for researchers and clients to shape the development of this new discipline.

This seminar can be seen as a further contribution to the growing awareness of the need for a more sensitive approach to the conservation of historic interiors. This was emphasized at the conferences recently held in Ottawa (Symposium 2000 – The Conservation of the Heritage Interiors) and Amsterdam (Manifestatie Historisch Interieur 2001). The one day conference Inspired by the Past, held in July 2001, organized by English Heritage and the Traditional Paint Forum not only provided an important reappraisal of the work of the eminent interior decorator John Fowler but also an assessment of how we investigate and present historic buildings today. At all of these conferences the role of architectural paint research was recognized as critical to gaining a full understanding of a building.

Ultimately we will only be able to assess whether the *Layers of Understanding* seminar was a success when the proposed guidelines and standards for architectural paint research are finally issued as a working document and prove to be a useful tool for the conservation of our historic buildings.

Helen Hughes
Senior Architectural Paint Researcher
English Heritage
February 2002

Session 1

Figure 2.2 Photomicrograph of cross-section of sample of paint from the wall plaster of a room of the 1750s. **See paper 2**

Figure 2.4 The Saloon at Boodle's following redecoration in 1996. © Country Life Picture Gallery. **See paper 2**

Figure 3.3 Battersea Bridge, London, 1993. **See paper 3**

Figure 3.4 Photomicrograph of a cross-section of a paint sample taken from Battersea Bridge. **See paper 3**

Figure 3.5 The Saloon, Audley End, the existing scheme dates from 1785. **See paper 3**

THE PANELLING: The North wall
THE NORTH DOOR

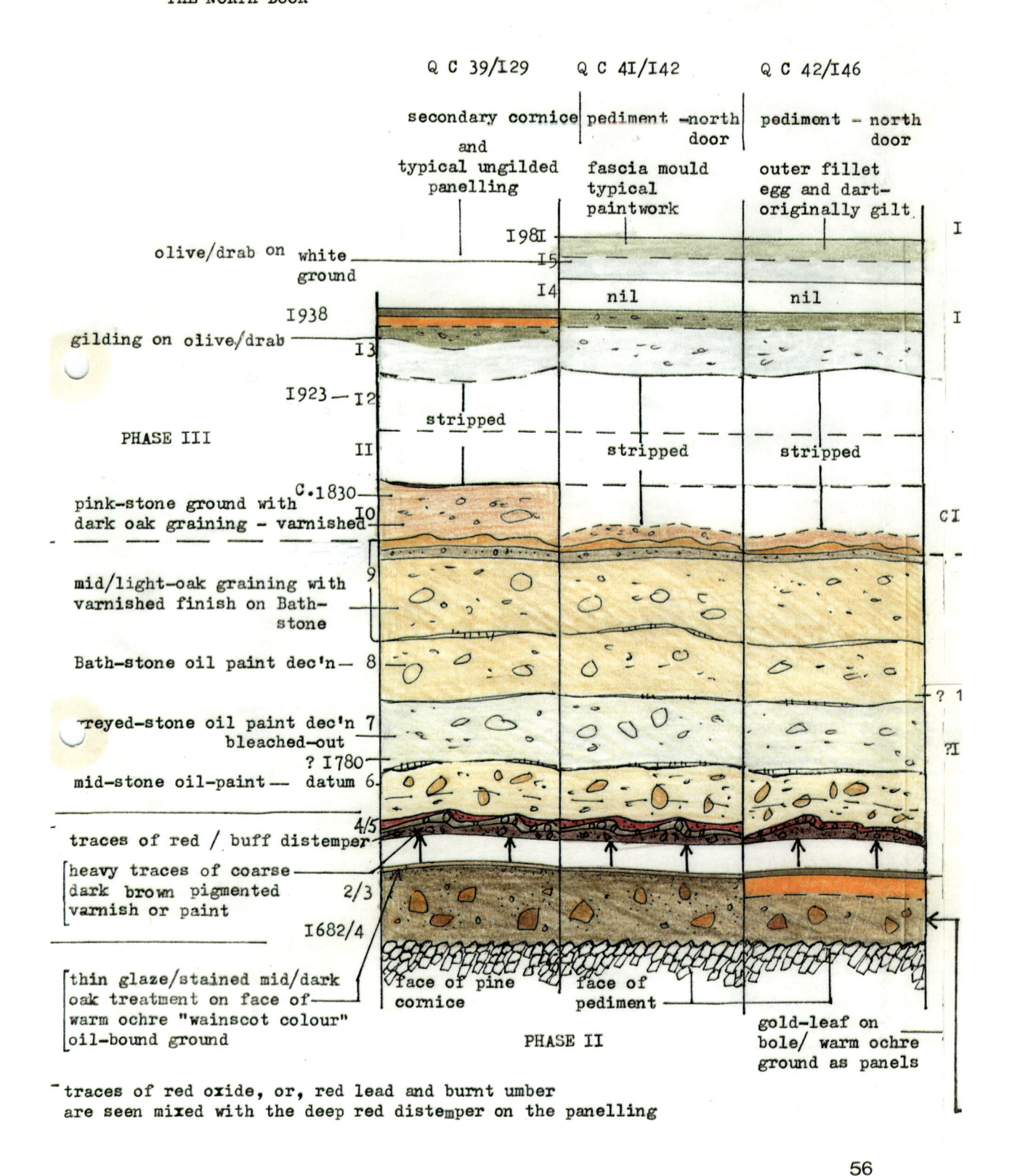

	Q C 39/I29	Q C 4I/I42	Q C 42/I46
	secondary cornice and typical ungilded panelling	pediment - north door fascia mould typical paintwork	pediment - north door outer fillet egg and dart- originally gilt

olive/drab on white ground — 1981 — I5

I4 — nil — nil

gilding on olive/drab — 1938 — I3

1923 — I2

PHASE III

stripped | stripped | stripped

II

pink-stone ground with dark oak graining - varnished — c.1830 — 10

mid/light-oak graining with varnished finish on Bath-stone — 9

Bath-stone oil paint dec'n — 8

greyed-stone oil paint dec'n bleached-out — 7

? 1780

mid-stone oil-paint — datum 6

traces of red / buff distemper — 4/5

[heavy traces of coarse dark brown pigmented varnish or paint] — 2/3

1682/4

[thin glaze/stained mid/dark oak treatment on face of warm ochre "wainscot colour" oil-bound ground]

face of pine cornice | face of pediment | gold-leaf on bole/ warm ochre ground as panels

PHASE II

— traces of red oxide, or, red lead and burnt umber
are seen mixed with the deep red distemper on the panelling

Figure 3.6 Diagram of the stratigraphy of mounted paint sample taken from the Queen's Chapel at St James' Palace, London, by Pamela Lewis in 1981. **See paper 3**

Introduction: Architectural Paint Research in a Wider Context

Kate Clark

I was asked to introduce this seminar not as an expert in architectural paint research, but as someone who has long sought to promote the importance of understanding buildings as a basis for conservation decisions. Too often understanding is seen as an academic luxury, rather than as an essential part of practical conservation, and as a result sites are damaged. Although the potential of architectural paint research in Britain is recognized, the subject nevertheless faces a series of challenges. As the number of practitioners increase, questions over quality begin to arise; there are calls for better training, and there is pressure to drive down costs. Users commission work with little understanding of what is being asked for, and when poor quality work is provided as a result, clients develop a bad opinion of the practice as a whole. Suddenly good practitioners with years of experience find themselves undercut by those with fewer skills and lower prices. Where good research is commissioned the valuable information provided concerning historic buildings may be lost as there is no system for the central archiving of reports. There is also a risk that new information will be seen as a commercial advantage and withheld, thus damaging the growth of the subject as a whole. Such practices ultimately impact on historic buildings, which, because their quality and significance have not been fully understood at the outset, are damaged through insensitive 'restoration'. This seminar offers an opportunity to bring together practitioners and users to identify a practical way forward.

It is important to be aware that many of the challenges outlined above are not unique to architectural paint research, which is one of a number of specialist disciplines with the potential to contribute to our understanding of historic buildings. These include:

- dendrochronology (tree-ring dating)
- building analysis (archaeology)
- documentary history of buildings
- architectural history
- wall paintings' analysis
- material analysis

Each of these disciplines has a number of things in common. Their practitioners form small, relatively isolated groups. They are seeking to apply academic disciplines or disciplines which have emerged in other contexts to the specific area of building conservation, and therefore to bridge academic and practical fields. The need to do so has been generated by a perception that without such work, historic buildings can be damaged. They are struggling to be accepted as an essential part of the conservation process, instead of an optional bolt-on. They are often commissioned using procedures designed to regulate prices in the construction industry rather than an academic discipline.

My aim in introducing this seminar is therefore to show how architectural paint research as a subject fits into this wider context, both intellectually and professionally. I also want to ask what lessons could be learnt from similar professions, dealing with similar issues.

Understanding buildings

In 1982 I undertook my first piece of architectural paint research. At the time I was working as a volunteer at Port Arthur, Tasmania, the site of one of Australia's most notorious penal colonies. The project involved archaeological investigation of the Commandant's

House. The initial work involved below-ground excavation, but it was suggested that the traditional archaeological technique of the stratigraphic matrix might also be relevant to the standing fabric of the building. Working in isolation, with as yet no knowledge of architectural paint research I nevertheless used basic archaeological techniques to analyse the paint layers in a room, and by linking these with the sequence of alteration using a matrix was able to reconstruct the decorative sequence of the interior. Although hardly rocket science, the exercise showed me that basic archaeological techniques designed to help make sense of the many tiny sequential layers in a complex deeply stratified archaeological excavation could easily be applied to buildings.[1]

Below-ground archaeology has over the past century or so developed a series of techniques which enable us to make sense of man-made sequences of events, using physical evidence. There are series of intellectual models – the idea of the *terminus post quem* and *terminus ante quem*; relative and absolute dating; context, phasing and typology, which can be used to refine these observations. They can also be tied to other types of data such as dendrochronological dates, documentary references or scientific investigations.

Although excavation seems a long way from architectural paint research, there is nevertheless much to be learnt from the process. Architectural paint research involves the analysis of layers of accumulated paint, taken from a large number of different areas. Establishing the decorative phases of an interior is not simply a matter of listing the paint layers found; there will be undercoats and top coats, and layers may be different either side of long since removed partitions. The sequence of physical changes to the room must be understood as part of the architectural paint research process. There may be documentary references to specific redecoration campaigns which may or may not be easy to tie to physical observations.

Establishing the decorative phases of a room or building is one issue, deciding how to represent a room or building is quite another. Although archaeology can contribute little to the technical analysis of materials used in the past, it can help to elucidate sequence, and place that technical information in a wider context. It is a language that helps us to 'read' complex physical evidence in a critical manner, as a historian reads a historical document.

The archaeology of buildings is not a new subject. It has its formal origins in the work of nineteenth-century figures such as Parker and Viollet le Duc, but certainly dates back to the Grand Tours of the eighteenth century and the study of the remains of classical antiquity. The tradition of buildings' archaeology continues today in the work of Warwick Rodwell, Tim Tatton-Brown, English Heritage's Historical Analysis and Research Team, Richard Morris, Richard Harris at the Weald and Downland Museum, Jason Wood and many others. There is no hard and fast line to be drawn between such work and architectural history, except that the buildings' archaeologist makes use of explicitly archaeological techniques in the analysis of fabric. Buildings' archaeology has been strongest in the study of church buildings,[2] although it is beginning to make a contribution to the study of 'polite' interiors – for example at Charles Darwin's Down House.[3]

It is in this field that there is the greatest potential for buildings' archaeology and architectural paint research to come together. Archaeologists have, in general, much to learn about architectural history and interior decoration. On the other hand, their techniques have the potential to provide a structure and rigour to the analysis of complex architecture, especially where there has been a sequence of alteration and change. Architectural paint researchers, working with buildings' archaeologists (and indeed documentary historians), can between them create a powerful synthesis of physical, documentary and technical evidence. Where such partnerships have come together, for example at Danson House (See paper 5) and at Sutton House,[4] the results can make a very significant contribution to the academic understanding of specific major buildings but also to architectural history as a whole.

The role of understanding in building conservation

Whilst architectural paint research may have the potential to make an important contribution to the academic study of architectural history, in practice, the vast majority of architectural paint research takes place within the context of building conservation projects. Typically, an architect wanting to take a decision – usually about restoration – will commission a programme of architectural paint research in order to help inform that decision. Whatever academic standards researchers may wish to abide by, they will often find themselves constrained by the timetable of the project, the demands of the architect and the need to cut costs down. They soon find standards compromised. Again, it is useful to draw upon the experience of other professions.

One of the main ways in which changes to historic sites or buildings are regulated is through the statutory planning system. *Planning Policy Guidance Note 16: Archaeology and Planning* (PPG 16) sets out very clearly the importance of making provision for archaeology when new developments are likely to threaten important sites.[5] Archaeologists may be called in to evaluate a site before it is developed, or to record remains which will be lost as a result of the new development.

The equivalent document for buildings in England is *Planning Policy Guidance Note 15: Planning and the Historic Environment* (PPG 15).[6] Again, the document makes clear the importance of understanding a building as the basis for informing change. It asks that applicants for Listed Building Consent provide the local authority with:[7]

> 3.4... *full information, to enable them to assess the likely impact of their proposals on the special architectural or historic interest of the building and its setting.*

Both documents emphasize that decisions about changes to historic buildings or sites should be based on the understanding of the sites.

Repairs to historic buildings do not usually require planning consent and so fall outside the statutory planning system. However, if an application for funding is made to one of the major funding bodies (for example, the Heritage Lottery Fund, English Heritage, Cadw or Historic Scotland) it is likely that the funding body will require certain standards to be met. In its guidance to applicants, English Heritage notes that:[8]

> *Understanding and interpreting the structure is an essential first step in repair work, creating an appropriate record of the work carried out is an important final stage in most building repair programmes. All grant-aided repairs will include a degree of archaeological recording.*

There is therefore a general presumption in both the statutory and non-statutory systems therefore, that changes to historic buildings should begin with an understanding of the sites and what is important about them.

The archaeological profession has largely dealt with these issues through standards for practitioners, guidance from statutory bodies and through sheer weight of numbers. There are now about a thousand archaeologists working in private practices as consultants, responding mainly to the needs of the development industry. In contrast there are relatively few architectural historians, building analysts or dendrochronologists meeting the needs of building conservation. Although archaeologists have published standards and guidance,[9,10] these have not necessarily gained acceptance with other professions, and there remain few common standards and much uncertainty.

The problem of 'restoration'

Perhaps one of the reasons behind the differences between below-ground archaeology and the analysis of buildings is that many conservation professionals are reluctant to make use of such techniques on buildings because of their association with restoration.

Many of the proto-buildings' archaeologists of the nineteenth century were associated with programmes of major rebuilding of historic monuments, such as cathedrals and churches. Their data was used to recreate rather than to retain historic fabric, during the process of which a great deal was lost. The reaction from Ruskin, William Morris and later Phillip Webb was strong:[11]

> *Do not let us talk then of Restoration. The thing is a Lie from beginning to end.*

There is an unspoken perception that that the purpose of understanding the sequence of change to a building is to provide information which will then enable the architect to 'restore' to one of those lost phases. The logical corollary is that if we don't understand the building, we can't restore it to an earlier phase. The approach of minimum intervention to buildings has resulted in a move away from understanding as it is not felt to be necessary. The result, as Richard Morris notes is that somewhere between the World Wars, archaeology and architectural conservation parted company.[12]

Buildings' archaeology is done – if it is done at all – like much below-ground archaeology in order to create a record of what is lost, rather than playing a positive role in informing conservation decisions. Thus a local primary authority may ask for a record of a building as a condition of consent to demolish or alter, rather than at an early stage to inform change. An architect supervizing a repair programme might make a small provision for the recording of masonry, which is to be dismantled and rebuilt. An investigation or survey of a building at an early stage to inform decisions about the proposed change or the appropriateness of the demolition or dismantling is rarely commissioned.

This approach ignores the fact that repairs or alterations to historic buildings damage fabric. Even the most careful repairs – repointing, minor timber replacement, consolidation of masonry – have the potential to damage historic fabric. The damage may be less that the whole-sale losses of the major nineteenth-century programmes, but we might argue that those buildings which have survived into our present age are very precious and deserve that much more care. Surely it is better to understand a building and why it is significant, and to use that understanding to inform a programme of work and to minimize damage, than to set out on the basis of no information to undertake work, which, however carefully it is done, will inevitably lead to losses.

The role of architectural paint research in conservation

This brings us back to the role of architectural paint research in the conservation process. The repair of a historic building, bringing it back into use perhaps, often involves major works to the interior. Typically surfaces will need to be prepared to take new finishes. Electrical and other services will be chased into plaster. There will be a debate about how to deal with alterations to the interior. Should the historic services be retained? Is the existing decorative scheme of any significance or should an earlier decorative scheme be carefully uncovered? Even if an original paint finish survives beneath layers of more modern paint, it may be patchy, discoloured and faded, quite unlike its appearance when first applied. What is the appropriate re-presentation option?

Architectural paint research cannot solve these problems alone – these are questions of design and conservation philosophy which can be addressed formally if needed through mechanisms such as the Conservation Plan.[13,14] What it can do however, is to provide a strong foundation for the decision-making process by providing a detailed understanding of the building.

An informed investigation of the successive decorations applied to an interior can reveal how the room or indeed the building as a whole, has been changed.

Unfortunately, like archaeology, architectural paint research is often commissioned for the wrong reasons. It is usually requested in order to find out what colour the room used to be and the information gained is often used solely as a glorified historic colour range chart simply to decide what colour to repaint the room. Those who commission architectural paint research should instead be asking 'how has this room or building changed through time?' and use that information intelligently to help define the whole conservation programme.

Informed conservation

For an archaeologist it is frustrating to see the same issues arise over and over again, in dendrochronology, in buildings' analysis, in architectural paint research and in historical research. It is also frustrating to see practitioners working in isolation from each other, rather than coming together to pool knowledge, techniques and resources. It is because the specialist analysts are isolated that they often carry so little weight in the conservation process.

Practitioners must find a way to come together in order to create a critical mass which will ensure that understanding is not a peripheral issue but is placed firmly at the centre of the conservation agenda. One of the difficulties in bringing such specialists together is the lack of a common term for what is, in a sense, conservation-based research or analysis. Buildings' archaeology, buildings' analysis, architectural paint research, architectural history, construction history, materials analysis or documentary history need to come together under a generic title which will create a single identity. Only then will such subjects gain recognition and an established place in the project management cycle. At the same time, it is important to address training. Architectural paint research is becoming a complex subject, and a recognized qualification is essential.

However, the provision of more qualified practitioners will not solve the problems faced by the profession. It is more important to train the users – the architects, engineers, project managers, craft builders, inspectors and conservation officers – who require architectural paint research in order to do their work. They need training to ensure they commission work effectively, and understand the strengths and weaknesses of the subject. They need to be able to know when and in what circumstances to make use of architectural paint research, how to identify and commission a specialist and what to do with the results of the work. Those who commission the work also need to ensure that provision is made for archiving and reporting, to make sure that work is available to future generations. Conservation professionals will need to be able to explain the value of such research to their own clients.

Ultimately, heritage bodies, conservation officers and conservation architects get the professionals they deserve. Unless they are prepared to commission work intelligently and carefully, they will find that the good practitioners have gone. It takes time to train a good architectural paint researcher – and indeed a good historian, building analyst, craftsman or dendrochronologist. The market place will not create these people. They need to be nurtured, supported and used appropriately. Without them the heritage will be the poorer.

Archiving and publication

Another lesson to be learnt from archaeology and allied disciplines is that of the need to publish. English Heritage is still catching up with the backlog of documentation which arose from the massive 'rescue archaeology' excavations in major town centres in the 1970s and 1980s. At the time little provision was made for publication, and as a result, there was a risk that huge amounts of data would never be written up or published.

Today documents such as MAP2 set out procedures for ensuring that all archaeological projects, whether funded by developers or through grant aid, include provision for creating a proper report and also for publication when this is appropriate.[15] Reports are archived in local Sites and Monuments Records offices or in the National Monuments Record in Swindon.

Buildings' analysts are gradually beginning to adopt similar practices. Too often buildings were drawn or analysed, but the results never pulled together into a report, let alone published. New desk instructions on grants in English Heritage should ensure that where such work takes place in the context of grant aided repair, then a proper report should be produced. Similar procedures are in place for dendrochronology commissioned by English Heritage, including a requirement that data are made publicly available.[16]

The proposed standard for architectural paint research (See paper 9) will begin to address similar issues. If the subject is to grow and mature, it is vital that every project includes a provision for making the research findings publicly available and not a matter of private commercial advantage.

Architectural paint research and interpretation

Architectural paint research is often a backroom subject in the conservation process. Yet the process of unravelling a building is an exciting one. Many owners of historic buildings find the results of architectural paint research or other analytical disciplines – particularly dendrochronology – absolutely fascinating, and it often helps them to appreciate the value of what they have.

It always seems a pity to confine such information to obscure reports, or 'grey literature' as it is now known. In Australia a number of building conservation projects have used the results of architectural paint research in their presentations to the public. At the Hyde Park Barracks in Sydney, the rooms on display to the public include partially revealed areas which provide a glimpse of earlier paint schemes, whilst a ghost staircase is marked out on a wall. The Francis Greenaway building is not presented to the public in a restored state but as a complex structure which has changed over time.

The little weatherboard officer's barracks at Eagle Hawk Neck, Port Arthur, Tasmania, which was converted into a private cottage is presented in a similar way. The many layers of wallpaper and paint that have been applied to the walls can be clearly seen. Again, the public sees a building that has changed through time, rather than a restored barracks.

These projects demonstrate that the public does not necessarily need 'restored' buildings in order to appreciate the past, and that it is possible both to retain the sequence of change to a building, and present that change to the public. The pattern of change is itself as interesting as the original building. Perhaps in Britain we could do more in the way we interpret sites to show the public how buildings change through time, and to include architectural paint research in the interpretative scheme.

Conclusions

The remainder of the papers come from those with far greater experience of the subject than I. They range from consultants with many years experience, to project managers and inspectors who tackle the application of architectural paint research in real projects. They demonstrate the range, depth and maturity of architectural paint research as a subject.

All too often architectural paint research is commissioned merely to create a colour chart. In fact the subject goes well beyond the mere matching of colours – the papers at the *Layers of Understanding* seminar demonstrate that within the history of paint is a microcosm of architectural history with the potential to overturn some of our most treasured assumptions.

But architectural paint research will have no future if we continue to strip all of the historic paint from our buildings. The internal decoration of historic buildings is an irreplaceable document that tells us about form, function and design.

I believe that architectural paint research can play a much bigger and more positive role in the conservation process but only if it moves from a small specialist discipline into being part of a multi disciplinary approach to understanding buildings. This means working with other analytical disciplines, and learning to share data and approaches. It also means educating others; in particular the architects, conservation officers, inspectors and most importantly owners, whose support and patronage will ensure the survival and growth of this hugely important discipline.

References

1. Davies, M., 'The Archaeology of Standing Structures', *Australian Journal of Historical Archaeology*, No 5, 1987 pp. 54–64.
2. Rodwell, W., *Church Archaeology*, Batsford, London, 1989.
3. Lea, R., Series of reports on Down House, held at the Historical and Architectural Research Team, English Heritage; Reports commissioned by English Heritage from Keystone Historic Building Consultants on Down House, held at the Historical and Architectural Research Team.
4. Belcher, V., Bond, R., Gray, M. and Wittrick, A., *Sutton House: A Tudor Courtier's House in Hackney*, English Heritage and The National Trust Monograph, forthcoming, 2002.
5. Department of National Heritage, *Planning Policy Guidance Note 16: Archaeology and Planning*, HMSO, London, 1990.
6. Department of the Environment, Transport and the Regions, Department of National Heritage, *Planning Policy Guidance Note 15: Planning and the Historic Environment,* HMSO, London, 1994.

7 Ibid. 3.4.
8 English Heritage, *Repair Work and Grants from English Heritage: Types of Work Which May Qualify*, English Heritage, London, 1994.
9 Institute of Field Archaeologists (IFA), *Standard and Guidance on the Investigation and Recording of Buildings*, IFA, Manchester, 2000.
10 Association of Local Government Archaeological Officers (ALGAO), *Analysis and Recording for the Conservation and Control of Works to Historic Buildings*, ALGAO, Chelmsford, 1997.
11 Ruskin, J., 'The Lamp of Memory', *The Seven Books of Architecture*, (1st edition), 1849, p. 180.
12 Morris, R., 'Buildings Archaeology', in Wood, J. (ed.), *Buildings Archaeology: Applications in Practice*, Oxbow, Oxford, 1994.
13 Kerr, J.S., *The Conservation Plan*, National Trust for New South Wales, Sydney, 2000.
14 Clark, K. (ed.), *Conservation Plans in Action*, English Heritage, London, 1999.
15 MAP2, English Heritage, 1991.
16 English Heritage, *Dendrochronology: Guidelines on Producing and Interpreting Dendrochronological Dates*, English Heritage, London, 1999.

Historic Overview

Ian Bristow

My interest in historic architectural colour goes back to my early experiences as an architect specializing in the conservation of historic buildings, when I inspected and was responsible for the repair of a number of churches containing medieval wall paintings, painted sixteenth-century monuments, and Victorian schemes of painted and stencilled decoration. To develop my knowledge I embarked on a series of experiments in tinting limewash using red and yellow ochres. In 1975 I was fortunate to be appointed Berger Research Fellow at the University of York, my defined task being to ascertain how paint colour was used in British interiors between 1660 and 1830.

At this date, John Fowler and John Cornforth had just published their joint book *English Decoration in the 18th Century*,[1] which with its chapter on 'Colour and the Painter's Craft' summarized current knowledge and thinking in fashionable circles. Otherwise one had principally to refer to the earlier work of Margaret Jourdain,[2] together with Edward Croft-Murray's more recent pair of volumes, *Decorative Painting in England 1537–1837*, dealing with fine-art painting in interiors.[3]

Looking at this corpus it seemed clear that a new line of enquiry was needed, and that a proper understanding of historic paint technology could unlock a vast amount of further data, while allowing improved understanding of already-known material. Accordingly, I divided my three years work at York into three broad phases, the first an examination and collation of as many historic treatises and manuscripts on house-painting materials and techniques as I could locate; while in the second I concentrated on the technical examination of surviving early paint in a series of carefully-selected rooms, with a view to defining their early schemes. Only once prepared by this firm groundwork did I embark on the third, the more conventional ordering of evidence from architects' design drawings, paintings, watercolour views of rooms, building accounts and similar material.

I cannot dwell now on my first phase of work, other than to say that it was modelled on Rosamond Harley's excellent book *Artists' Pigments c. 1600–1835*.[4] My emphasis was, however, on house-paint, a subtly different topic requiring somewhat different qualities in the materials used, and extension beyond those she considered. By way of exemplifying my sources I will mention the most vital of the printed works of the period, John Smith's *Art of Painting*,[5] the first edition of which appeared in 1676, followed by a second much expanded and revised edition in 1687, which went into a number of further printings (Figure 2.1). I will also instance Lewis Berger's sample book, part of a remarkable manuscript archive to which little attention had hitherto been paid.[6] I was, moreover, able to extend beyond Rosamond Harley's purely documentary approach by experimenting with materials of the period (many of which I had to make myself from a range of raw substances, most obsolete and only obtained with some ingenuity), the end product being a series of charts showing the range of colours available at different dates.

In an era before the desktop personal computer, collation of my material was on card index. Two research reports led to my doctoral thesis of 1983, 'Interior House-painting from the Restoration to the Regency'; and the consolidated and expanded result of my initial technical studies is now available as *Interior House-painting Colours and Technology 1615–1840*.[7] This gives a comprehensive account of the materials used between 1615 and 1840, together with an explanation of the way they were made up into paint and applied, supplemented by illustrated glossaries of colour mixes and imitative effects.

To return to the period of my York research fellowship, the technical information I had amassed proved vital for my second phase of work, duly enabling me to release a vast store of archaeological evidence hitherto largely untapped in any properly reliable way. In embarking on this, I was greatly aided by the Victoria and Albert Museum, whose microscope and technical facilities were made available to me. There, Jo Darrah, when Senior Scientist, had gained experience in the first half on the 1970s in applying to rooms at Ham House and Osterley Park, the mounted cross-section technique which had been developed by Joyce Plesters at the National Gallery for the examination of pictures. This had already shown the unreliability of the traditional 'scrape', which involved the exposure of early paint using a pen-knife or chemical paint-stripper, and examination of the results using a hand-lens. Despite the seductive simplicity of this process, my own trials in a late seventeenth-century house in Rugby Street immediately confirmed how untrustworthy the results were in practice, significant layers of similar colour being too easily missed, and the eye often beguiled by more attractive or assertive colours in a sequence.

A classic example was the Music Room at Kedleston, an interior, I am glad to say, since repainted by The National Trust after it took responsibility for the building, which at the time of my fellowship was presented to me as exhibiting a restoration of its original colours. Unhappily for this claim, a cross-section immediately revealed earlier, more subtle schemes beneath the deep red on which redecoration had seemingly been based. From the start, I was thus led to be deeply suspicious of assertions based on 'scrapes'; and, despite its demands in terms of time, adopted the mounted cross-section, which I consider to have rendered the latter obsolete.

In essence, a cross-section is prepared by removing a small sample of paint with a minute amount of the substrate attached. This is then embedded in a block of colourless resin and ground to expose the sequence of paint layers for viewing under an optical microscope. The superior results obtainable are particularly well exemplified by a sample of paint from the wall plaster of a room of the 1750s (Figure 2.2). It was sent to me very early in my research with the suggestion that it was of interest since surface scraping had revealed a red primer at the bottom, followed by a white undercoat, and a pale grey finish. Certainly one could see this succession under the microscope, but the mounted cross-section showed much more. There was not one layer of white, but five; and not one layer of grey, but three. My suspicions that the grey was not the first finish were thus aroused, and I was led to look more closely at the red which had been supposed to be a primer. Not only was this clearly much thicker than the overlying layers, but it also had a rather translucent appearance under the microscope. This would be typical of a distemper (whiting bound with animal-glue

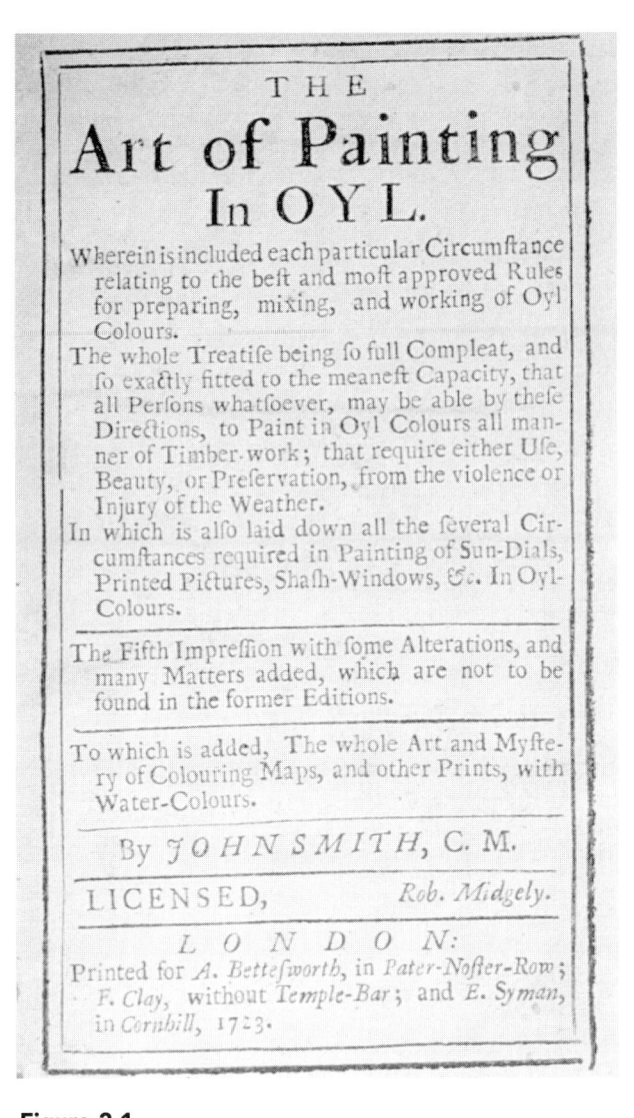

Figure 2.1
Title page from John Smith's *Art of Painting*, 5th edition, 1723.

size) rather than an oil paint; and a simple staining test on the cross-section proved positive for protein, indicating most probably in the context of a house-paint, the presence of an animal-glue-size binder. Most significantly, the surface of the red layer could be seen to have faded in places, arguing the presence of a fugitive, organic red pigment which had been exposed to light for a significant length of time. I was thus led to conclude that, rather than being a primer, it was in fact the earliest scheme of decoration, a bright pink executed in a distemper medium.

Now this was a simple and particularly clear example, but one is more often faced by an extended series of schemes which have to be unravelled. To illustrate this, I instance the sequence of layers on the cornice in the North Drawing Room at the Mansion House, London, representing 24 phases of decoration between 1751 (the date of the painter's contract) and 1987 (when I took the samples) (Figure 2.3). Although most of the layers are of a somewhat similar colour, the microscope allowed recognition of many individual characteristics; and, by taking a series of 134 samples

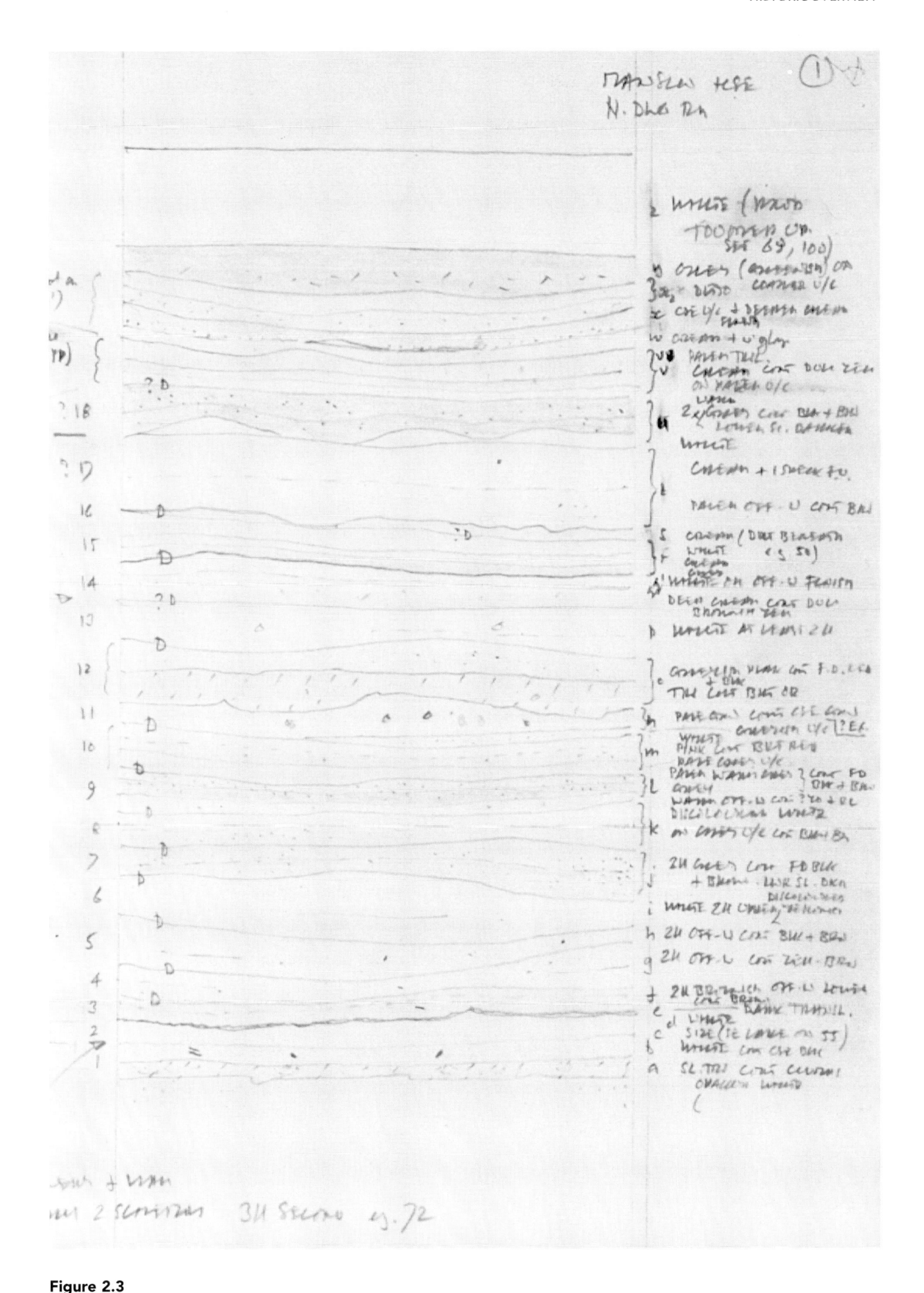

Figure 2.3
Annotated sketch of cross-section of paint from the cornice in the North Drawing Room at the Mansion House, London.

from the room and critically examining the layers present, it was possible to unravel each and every scheme.

Just above the middle of the sequence, six successive schemes involved the gilding of certain cornice elements. In fact, there were only five layers of gilding, since on the penultimate occasion the gold had been picked around, so that the layers I denominated (q) and (q') from the main sequence do not appear on areas already gilded in connection with the previous scheme. Not only would one have had no chance at all of spotting this on a 'scrape', but in the course of the six schemes the disposition of the gilding was varied, so that on two samples only four schemes of gilding appear. Painstaking collation of these showed that while some had the first four schemes, others had the last four: again there would have been no possibility of seeing such detail on a 'scrape'. On another element, only three gilding schemes were present, which, minute inspection revealed, comprised the last two with an intermediate touch-up contemporary with the scheme formed by layers (q) and (q') and generally involved only the picking of white around the existing gold.

By examining with such care a series of cross-sections, I was thus able to unravel subtle changes in the gilding schemes at successive phases; and I have gone into this at some length in order to demonstrate the power of the technique. Applying it to a series of rooms had allowed me in the middle phase of my fellowship to re-assess a number which had, as it turned out, the misleading reputation of retaining their original schemes (these included, for instance, the Balcony Room at Dyrham and the Saloon at Uppark); while others yielded a gold-mine of information about eighteenth-century colour. Twenty-five years later it seems quite extraordinary that such a valuable investigative tool is still often greeted with deep suspicion; but this is perhaps inevitable in a country like the United Kingdom, where technical methods and knowledge continue far too often to be viewed as mere alchemy.

I would stress, however, that I have always viewed this technical work as a means to an end, and have never lost sight of the fact that my interest has, throughout, been directed at achieving a clear understanding of the use of colour in historic interiors. Besides the accumulation of firm data on a series of historic examples, the two first phases of research allowed a much greater comprehension of the more conventional evidence used by the architectural historian. Technical terms and expressions in building accounts could be correctly interpreted: for instance, while looking at an Adam drawing, it was possible to recognize tints familiar through knowledge of contemporary colour-formulation practice. One need only glance at his design of 1769 for David Garrick's Drawing Room in the Adelphi to see the distinctive hues of blue and green verditer; a green mixed using Prussian blue with yellow; bright pinks containing cochineal lakes; and darker red-browns based on the mixture of red ochre with black, all now old friends to me. Combining such insight with more conventional evidence in the form of literary and similar references allowed me in my thesis in 1983 to produce a coherent outline of the historic use of colour; and, in parallel with the technical volume which I have already mentioned, in 1996 I published *Architectural Colour in British Interiors 1615–1840*, giving a summary of the aesthetic ends to which colour was put over the period 1615–1840.[8]

Through my work I have been able to redecorate a number of rooms in their original colours, even where, as in the case of the Saloon at Boodle's (Figure 2.4), much of the physical record had been lost through paint stripping, since a developed understanding of the forms, concepts and conventions of the 1770s allowed extrapolation to cover the *lacunae*.

Throughout the last two decades, there has been a steady increase of interest in historic interiors, with many people entering the field; and, while my brief in this paper has been to set a context, the *Layers of Understanding* seminar is very much about looking to the future of the technical investigation of historic paintwork. If asked to define the task before us, I think I would reply that it is to manage the change from what was essentially a postgraduate research topic to a routine procedure, carried out to high standards. Second-rate or inaccurate investigative work will serve only to obfuscate our understanding of the past, and it is self-evident that we owe a duty to both scholars and the general public to produce consistently results of the highest possible accuracy.

References

1. Cornforth, J. and Fowler, J., *English Decoration in the 18th Century*, 1974.
2. Jourdain, M., (pseud. Francis Lenygon), *Decoration in England from 1660 to 1770*, 1914. Jourdain, M., English *Decoration and Furniture of the Later XVIIIth Century (1750–1820)*, 1922.
3. Croft-Murray, E., 'Decorative Painting in England 1537–1837', *Country Life*, Vol 1, London, 1962; Vol 2, Feltham, Middlesex, 1970.
4. Harley, R., *Artists' Pigments c. 1600–1835: A Study in English Documentary Sources*, 1970.
5. Smith, J., *Art of Painting*, 1676.
6. Berger, L., manuscript at Hackney Archives Department, Rose Lipman Library, London, catalogued as D/B/BER1/2/1.
7. Bristow, I. C., *Interior House-painting Colours and Technology 1615–1840*, Yale University Press, New Haven and London, 1996.
8. Bristow, I. C., *Architectural Colour in British Interiors 1615–1840*, Yale University Press, New Haven and London, 1996.

The Problems Facing the Development of Architectural Paint Research

Helen Hughes

What is architectural paint research?

I normally present papers which illustrate the potential of architectural paint research in glowing terms, with tales of chance discoveries, long lost archives, amazing survivals of aged finishes, all illustrated with technicolour cross-sections. However, now I will present the darker reality of the current state of architectural paint research in Britain. I will discuss the problems that I feel are hampering the development of the subject and are ultimately jeopardizing the conservation of our historic interiors.

Architectural paint research is a research discipline that needs to be clearly defined. At the moment the term can mean all things to all men. I use the term architectural paint research to describe the synthesis of the study of historic documentation and archaeological evidence, with a particular focus on surviving paintwork and decorative finishes to clarify the decorative history of an architectural element or exterior or interior. It is a research tool that offers a detailed insight into the development of our buildings. In decorative terms, this research helps establish exactly what was carried out within an historic interior, and as such has great potential in the field of the history of interior design. At last, vague generalizations concerning historic decorations can be reviewed against an ever-increasing body of well-documented case studies.

There are often vast quantities of documentary evidence relating to specific buildings, such as house-painters accounts, inventories, contemporary descriptions, sketches, watercolours and photographs which offer an insight in to changes carried out within interiors. The Dining Room at Kenwood House was redecorated in 1815. Works accounts from that period, including references to 'Walls painted in oil in pannals with corner ornaments', were extremely valuable in directing the removal of paint samples from this area (Figure 3.1). Without this information it is unlikely that the delicate *trompe l'oeil* painting of this early scheme would have been discovered (Figure 3.2).

Buildings frequently undergo major structural alterations and repairs. All documentation and physical evidence of these changes should be examined as part of any paint research investigation. Such preliminary research proved invaluable when investigating Sir William Chambers' Temple of Bellona in Kew Gardens. The late eighteenth-century garden temple had been dismantled and moved to another part of the park where it had been rebuilt with substantial alterations in the mid-nineteenth century. The fact that very little of the original structure remained could be predicted from this desktop survey. Such preliminary assessments are a vital part of any good architectural paint research programme, and is essential for the planning of a coherent paint sampling strategy.

The accumulated layers of paint found in our historic buildings can provide evidence of the paint colours used at various periods, but they can tell us so much more. These layers can pinpoint developments in paint technology, indicate structural modifications made to buildings, as well as providing some insight into the fortunes and aspirations of successive occupants. The paint sequence found on each element provides a profile unique to each particular element. On a wider scale, the paint samples removed from Battersea Bridge revealed not only the decorative history of this particular bridge, but reflected the history of the city of London, an elaborate gilded scheme applied to celebrate a coronation, and camouflage applied during the two World Wars (Figures 3.3 and 3.4).

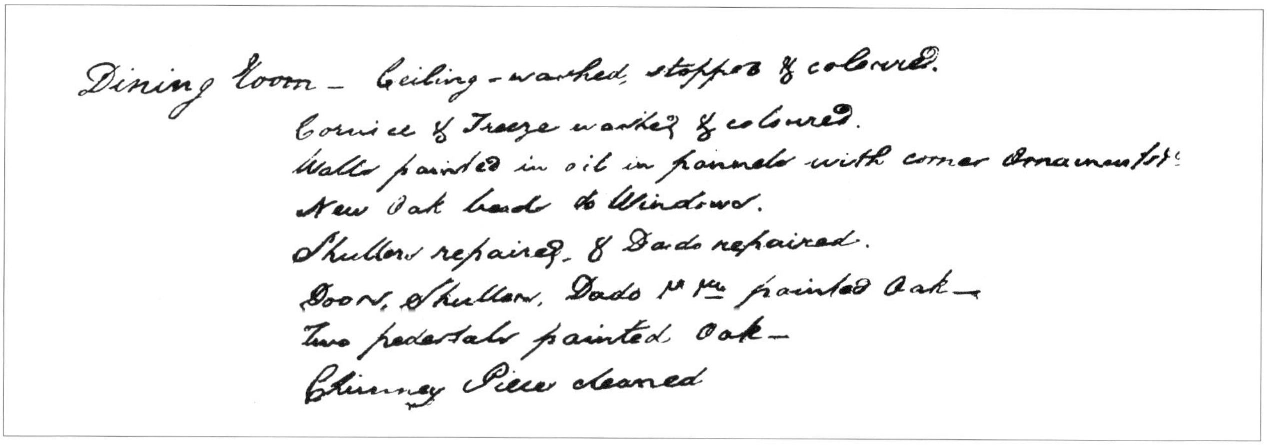
Dining Room – Ceiling – washed, stopped & coloured.
Cornice & Freeze washed & coloured.
Walls painted in oil in pannels with corner Ornaments.
New Oak beads to Windows.
Shutters repaired & Dado repaired.
Doors, Shutters, Dado &c &c painted Oak –
Two pedestals painted Oak –
Chimney Piece cleaned

Figure 3.1
Extract from a works account of 1815 referring to the new decoration of the Dining Room, Kenwood House 'Walls painted in oil in pannals with corner ornaments'. Scottish Record Office EXTD79/104 Bundle 975 © The Earl of Mansfield

Our historic buildings are a finite resource, which we hope to preserve for centuries to come. Surely then, the first step in the conservation management of these buildings is gaining a full understanding of their development and their present condition: 'Without understanding, conservation is blind and meaningless'.[1] The wide range of building investigation procedures, such as building analysis, dendrochronology and architectural history need to be more fully used and integrated in the process of gaining understanding. Some of English Heritage's most successful conservation programmes have been based on research carried out by multidisciplinary teams working together, sharing findings and observations as the research work progressed. (For an example of the use of collaborative research with reference to recent works carried out at Danson House, see paper 5.)

No one argues against the principle of attempting to understand buildings fully before undertaking any alterations. There are numerous charters and conservation plan advisory literature in which this principle is repeated mantra-like. However when it comes to actual practice and real-life projects, this advice is abandoned and conservation policy tends to be dictated by funding constraints, contract schedules and deadlines. All too often projects are run by major contractors who have no experience or understanding of the most basic of conservation principles.

Compared with building and redecoration costs, which may run into millions of pounds, the costs of undertaking building analysis and architectural paint research are minimal. The insight gained by such research has in many cases suggested preferred options which actually reduced building and redecoration costs. In most cases the knowledge gained is priceless, and the new understanding of the building becomes a powerful tool in ensuring the preservation of rare archaeological evidence which otherwise might have been easily destroyed or obliterated. Research in the Saloon at Audley End established that the existing decoration dated from 1785 and ensured that the rare scheme was carefully conserved and preserved (Figure 3.5).

Why is architectural paint research not a routine procedure in building conservation?

Four main problems are hampering the development of architectural paint research:

- There is a lack of understanding of the subject, its potential, and how it should be implemented.
- Programming of projects is poor and there is very little funding for research.
- There is no training for architectural paint research consultants or even more importantly, no training provision for clients and monitoring bodies who commission this type of research.
- There is no agreed methodology or standard for the subject.

Lack of understanding

Is architectural paint research required every time a significant historic building or interior is being redecorated? In many cases the reinstatement of an historic scheme may be entirely inappropriate for the current use of the building. Indeed it could be argued that the exact recreation of historic schemes is only appropriate in historic house museums. However in some historic interiors it could be argued that the reinstatement of the original decorative scheme does enhance our appreciation of the building.

Figure 3.2
The *trompe l'oeil* corner ornaments of the Dining Room, Kenwood House being revealed beneath layers of overpaint.

However, if paint research findings are not required for the current project, there should be no obligation to carry out this type of investigation every time a room is to be redecorated. Indeed a room may be repainted in whatever manner is considered appropriate for its modern use by the owner, as long as this conforms with statutory requirements pertaining to that building. We should continue the centuries-old tradition of painting our buildings to suit our current tastes and lifestyles. But, before this is executed, it is important that some assessment of the existing decorative finishes is carried out to ensure that there is no irreversible loss of evidence, and that a significant decorative scheme is not being obliterated by new paint. This assessment may well involve an element of architectural paint research.

More importantly, we should ensure that paint stripping is not destroying the archaeological evidence of underlying paint layers. Perhaps we should even consider whether the process of paint stripping, which is routinely carried out as standard practice, even in major historic buildings, should require some type of Listed Building Consent? Architectural paint research at the present time should perhaps be more concerned with the preservation of archaeological evidence of early paint layers than suggesting colour palettes for redecoration schemes. The Pillar Parlour at Bolsover Castle, Derbyshire is one example of where inappropriate stripping destroyed an extremely rare decorative scheme which had survived unaltered since the early seventeenth century.

The misunderstanding of the subject often begins with the very conservation bodies which impose the requirement that architectural paint research be carried out. Often the caseworkers of such organizations have little idea of the principles or purpose of architectural paint research. We should ensure that any regulatory body, whether it is the Heritage Lottery Fund or English Heritage, or a local authority, which is imposing a requirement for paint research, is obliged to state the purpose and scope of the research. Clear instructions should be provided on how the research should be assessed and monitored, and how the research findings are to be delivered. As long as such bodies continue to employ imprecise terms such as 'paint scrapes' or 'paint scrape analysis', we cannot hope to improve standards.

If the owners of an historic building are instructed to carry out unspecified architectural paint research, without the objectives of the research being clearly explained, it is understandable that they may well regard the whole exercise as rather meaningless. The reaction may well be 'Time consuming, expensive and inconclusive – why bother?'

Programming and funding

Ideally the regulatory and grant giving bodies should be well aware of the importance of building research, and be familiar with procedures of architectural paint research. They should ensure that preliminary research is funded, carried out and assessed well in advance of any proposed works programme. Hopefully in the future, enlightened bodies will refuse to fund building conservation programmes which have not been adequately researched.

It is becoming increasingly common for architectural paint research to be carried out at the same time as the very works programme it is supposed to inform. The main contractor is ready on site with a series of set instructions before the researcher has even been appointed. In such cases a building which may have been untouched for years and retains masses of archaeological evidence (and who knows what wonderful documentary material is held in the local records office?), has to be processed and re-presented within a very short period, and always before the end of the financial year. Although the illogicality of this process is recognized, this scenario is repeated again and again. This is because it is almost impossible to secure funding for architectural paint research that is independent of a works project.

Building analysis and architectural paint research often highlight a whole range of presentation options for a room or building. Such research may identify an original scheme, long since obliterated, or the hitherto unknown significance of an existing scheme. Ideally these options should be assessed calmly during the pre-works phase without the pressures of contractual deadlines, and contractors anxious not to cause delays and incur penalty payments. All too often it is the demands of the contract rather than the needs of the building which are given priority.

In some cases the need to spend the funding becomes the main priority of the project. In one recent case it was discovered that a workforce with time on their hands were put to work 'tidying up'. Poorly briefed and monitored, they had already removed all the original fittings, and were half way through stripping the paint from the remaining elements before work was halted. The irony of this is that in this case it was the rarity of these very fittings and historic paint finishes which had attracted the funding from the Heritage Lottery Fund in the first instance.

Let us follow the stages in the life cycle of a typical paint research project. We will start with the client, who may be the building's owner, the curator, the project manager, or supervizing architect, who on top of all their other worries finds themselves suddenly burdened by an obligation to carry out 'architectural paint research' or 'paint scrapes'. I often receive telephone calls from distracted project managers asking for advice. In one case an architect claimed he had been told that he had 'to commission scanning electron microscopy and analyse the colour and composition of every layer of paint'. Faced with such garbled and ludicrously imprecise instructions where can the client look for guidance?

The project manager now demoralized and with very little enthusiasm seeks out an architectural paint research specialist who they hope will solve all their problems. The project manager may now feel distrustful and powerless, sure that some 'white-coated boffin' is going to charge a ridiculous amount of money to establish an authentic colour scheme they will most certainly dislike.

Such clients generally respond in one of three ways. Client Type One, without any project brief, will approach an architectural paint research consultant and ask for 'some paint scrapes'. There is a naive hope on the part of the client that the consultant will be working to some nationally approved standard. Of course the client will rarely ask to see examples of the researcher's work, copies of earlier reports or even ask for references. No project brief will be agreed and the type of service provided is left entirely to the discretion of the researcher. This is clearly a case of 'buyer beware'.

Client Type Two is so fearful and distrustful of the whole process that, without any experience of architectural paint research, he attempts to over-manage the whole project. This client stipulates the exact number and location of the paint samples to be taken. The paint specialist is asked to give a price for the research based on the number of samples that will be removed from the building. In some cases, the researcher will be asked to identify the pigmentation and media in all layers, regardless of whether this information is relevant. Such contracts are extremely limiting and hamper good research. Any experienced architectural paint researcher would refuse to work within such constraints. A good researcher would probably achieve the project objectives much more efficiently and economically, if allowed to work using his/her own tried and tested methodology.

Client Type Three actually wants imprecise architectural paint research. On one recent project, the client stated that he commissioned 'limited paint research' because he 'did not wish to establish the historic colours in case they were too strong'. In fact what he feared was that if the details of the original scheme were determined, some conservation body would impose the reinstatement of the original colours. So the investigation of a very important eighteenth-century public building was restricted to a few paint scrapes and the examination of two mounted samples, which was carried out by an obliging 'paint researcher/conservator', who then proceeded to strip the historic paint from the ornate mouldings. When challenged as to whether the paint stripping was appropriate, the client then replied that the paint had been 'fully recorded by the architectural paint researcher'. So here we have a 'perfect team', an architect who does not really want to understand the building because he wants to design his own scheme, and the 'paint scraper' who meets the brief exactly, by establishing nothing. The tragedy of this case was the destruction of evidence of early eighteenth-century decorative finishes in a very important building.

Training of architectural paint researchers, commissioning clients and monitoring bodies

There are very few experienced architectural paint research specialists and without doubt the development of the discipline is severely hampered by poor research produced by consultants who have no experience or training but are happy to offer 'paint research'.

The Heritage Lottery Fund, English Heritage, The National Trust and various conservation policy documentation such as PPG 15, all advocate the use of architectural paint research. This has created a demand that cannot be met by the few experienced researchers currently working in the United Kingdom. This gap in the market has been spotted, and we now have a wide spectrum of so-called 'paint researchers' who are prepared to conduct this type of research.

Such 'paint researchers' range from large analytical laboratories to interior designers. The large laboratories normally conduct research on modern industrial paints, and will readily admit to having little interest in historic buildings or historic painting materials. But they will accept paint samples sent through the post and for a fee will measure the thickness and basic composition of each paint layer. There will be no attempt to relate the findings to the development of the building from which the samples were taken. At the other end of the spectrum there are interior designers and paint specifiers who are not interested in paint as archaeology, but may wish to use a discoloured paint scrape as a source of inspiration for a new scheme. Modern designers are principally interested in developing their own vision of the historic interior and creating interiors which appeal to contemporary tastes.

A great deal of architectural paint research is now being carried out by fine art conservators, who although aware of modern research procedures in their own field, have a limited understanding of architectural conservation issues or even the techniques and materials used by house painters. Most concentrate exclusively on the paint and really have little interest in the history of the room or the wider context of the building.

Despite the fact that the use of 'paint scrapes', the stepped revealing of small areas of earlier paint layers on site, has been shown to be a highly inaccurate and misleading method of analysis it is still commonly employed. The practice of accepting paint samples sent by post is also questionable. What is the value of this type of analysis? Why bother to incur the expense of this meaningless research?

Paint scrapes offer no lasting value whereas a set of carefully recorded mounted paint samples extends the documentation of a building. Paint samples removed from the Queen's Chapel at St James' Palace London by Pamela Lewis, who established the Architectural Paint Research Unit at English Heritage over twenty years ago, remain a valuable research resource. The location of all of the samples was carefully recorded and the mounted cross-sections stored in our archives can be called up and re-appraised at any time (Figure 3.6).

Methodology – architectural paint research reports

Of the wide range of those offering architectural paint research services, there are very few who ask for advice and guidance from established researchers.

Inexperienced researchers are often too involved in the technicalities of pigment and media analysis. There is a tendency to forget that the main aim of conducting the research is to obtain an understanding of the building's decorative development, and convey this information to the commissioning client in a clear and accessible manner.

A good architectural paint research report should read like an interesting story. We all understand the motivations behind building, decorating, and redecorating our own houses, and there is no reason why the report should not be couched in those terms. Poor paint research reports come in all shapes and sizes; some are generally very disorganized, usually without any introduction, and launch into the specifics of pigment identification with no mention of where the pigment particle in question is located. Some reports are obviously amateurish, while others are extremely glossy and apparently authoritative, containing technical terms that are never explained. Such reports are designed to intimidate rather than inform. But what these reports have in common is a tendency to tail off rather limply without making any firm conclusions and may even suggest that further research is required.

So the commissioning client is often disappointed when finally the architectural paint research report arrives, because it offers them very little. The client often does not understand the report because it is too scientific or technical. In most cases the fault does not lie with the clients abilities, or lack of understanding, but the fact that the report is often unintelligible and illogical. Instead of pressing analysts to explain their findings, most clients pay the bill, put the unread report in a drawer, and firmly resolve never again to commission architectural paint research.

Solutions – how can we improve this state of affairs?

First of all I would suggest that we must educate architectural conservation professionals at all levels. Perhaps we should insist that all conservation architects, curators and others involved with the development of historic decorative schemes, should undergo training and obtain a certificate of competency in this field before they are allowed to manage this type of project. English Heritage is planning to run a series of courses to provide project managers with training in the commissioning of architectural paint research. The first course will be offered at West Dean College in October 2001, as one of the Building Conservation Masterclasses, run in collaboration with the Edward James Foundation and the Weald and Downland Open Air Museum.

We clearly need to make provision for the training of architectural paint research specialists. I suggest an internship programme to provide practical on-site project-based training with established researchers. Hopefully this would generate a body of trainees who would then go on to develop their own consultancies. Perhaps we could establish joint schemes between English Heritage, Historic Scotland, The National Trust, private paint specialists, and similar bodies in Europe and the USA. Such a scheme would require funding.

It should be borne in mind that the few experienced architectural paint specialists we have in England already find themselves so constrained by inappropriate contracts and poor programming that they can rarely use their full range of skills. Indeed, some feel so compromised and disillusioned by the current situation that despite their scarce skills, some researchers are on the point of giving up the subject. If we are to train more architectural paint researchers we must ensure that the methodology they adopt and adhere to is fully recognized and accepted as a national or perhaps even international standard.

A common definition of the discipline needs to be established. To this end English Heritage has produced a draft standards document 'Proposed Guidelines for Commissioning Architectural Paint Research' (See paper 9). Readers are encouraged to offer any comments they wish on this draft (comments to: helen.hughes@english-heritage.org.uk). This is an opportunity to shape and nurture the development of architectural paint research, I hope you will take it.

References

1 Clark, K., *Informed Conservation*, English Heritage, London, 2001.

Figure 4.1 (left) Photomicrograph of initial red-brown coatings on an early eighteenth-century door at x 200 magnification.

Figure 4.2 (bottom left) Patrick Baty sampling above a 40 ft (15m) drop.

Figure 4.3 (bottom right) Portable Spectrophotometer being used to measure the colour of a dado.

See paper 4

Figure 5.1 Exterior view of Danson House. **See paper 5**

Figure 5.2 Round plaster plaque found in a side passage in 1997. **See paper 5**

Figure 5.3 (left) Photomicrograph of a cross-section of a paint sample taken from the round plaster plaque in the side passage.

Figure 5.4 (bottom left) Photomicrograph of a cross-section of a paint sample taken from the elliptical plaque in the Library.

Figure 5.5 (bottom right) Photomicrograph of a cross-section of a paint sample taken from re-plastered wall face above the chimney in the Library.

See paper 5

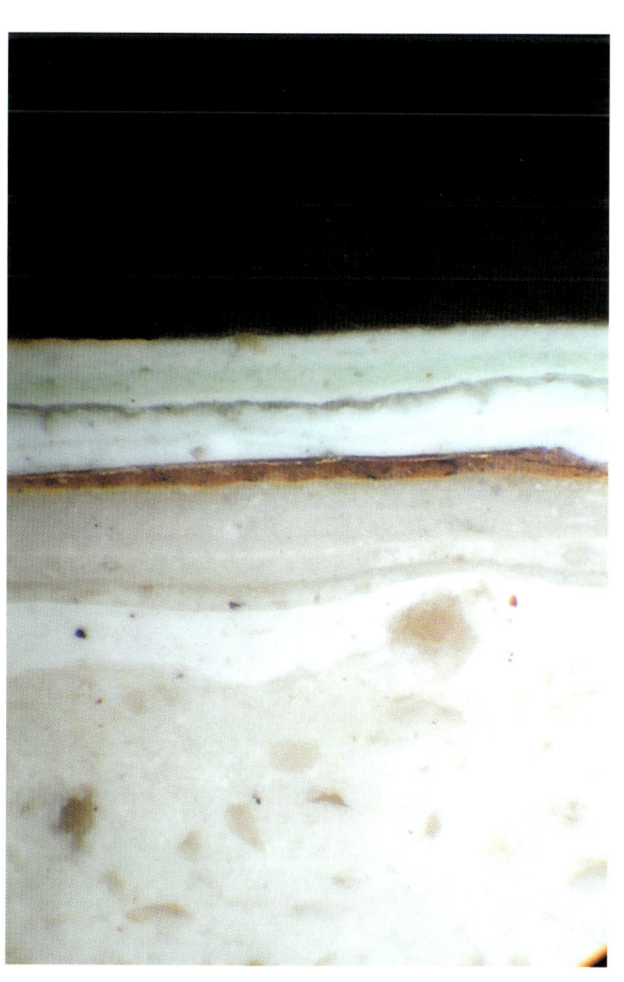

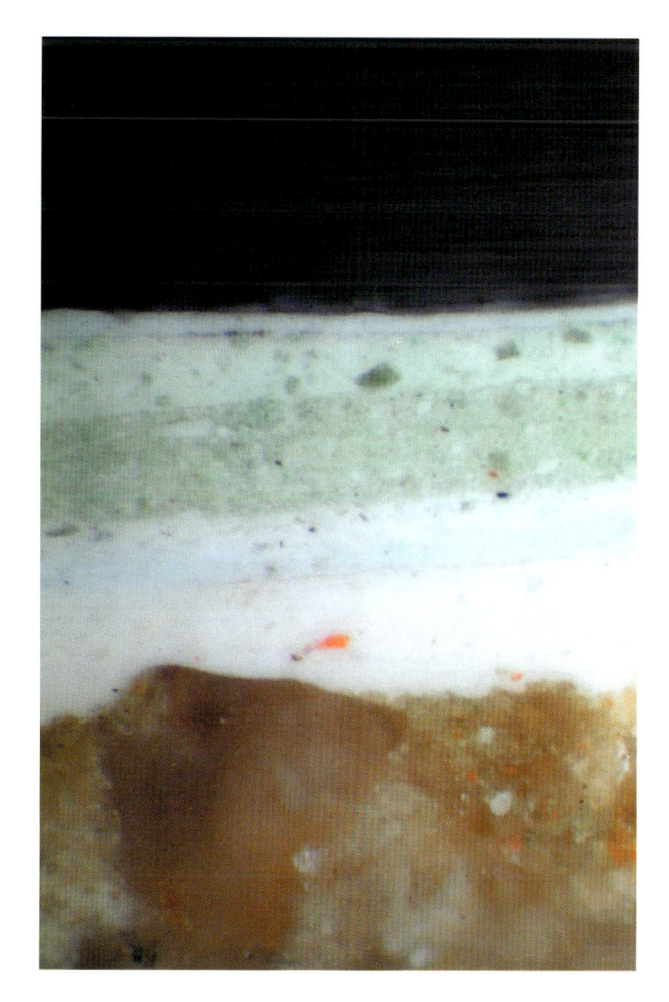

Figure 5.6 Area above the chimney in the Library prior to investigation in 1997.

Figure 5.7 The round plaque reinstated above the chimney in the Library.

Figure 5.8 The Library following partial redecoration.
See paper 5

Session 2

Some Tips on Commissioning Paint Analysis

Patrick Baty

Architectural Paint Research has progressed enormously in the sixteen years that I have been involved in the field. It is increasingly understood that properly conducted analysis can reveal a great deal of information about a room's decoration, development and use. However, there is still some confusion about how such work should be commissioned and carried out.

The aim of this paper is to provide a number of tips to the potential client in order that he may get the best out of his project. It should go without saying, that when one employs a paint researcher it is essential to ensure that he is capable of carrying out the job. How does he intend to set about it? What projects has he worked on in the past? What techniques does he propose to use?

Scrapes

The first thing to stress is that a paint scraper, or 'scrapist', will not be able to provide any meaningful information about the sequence of paint layers applied to a surface. Pigment identification, the dating of individual schemes, and the ability to identify (for example) exactly which cornice elements were gilded, and at what stage, are not possible by scraping through layers of paint. It should be understood that a 'scrape' in this context is the action of scraping away overlying layers of paint in order to see what lies below. An 'exposure' or 'revelation' is the scraping away of superficial layers, having established the stratigraphy by cross-section beforehand. This is done in order to provide further information about the earlier schemes. A white-coated lab technician, on the other hand, may be able to provide an elemental analysis of each of the components within a paint layer, but will not necessarily understand the appearance of a scheme, nor the intention behind its use.

The argument against scrapes has been well rehearsed.[1,2,3,4,5] No literature outlining their benefits is known, though, incredibly, the practice is still very much alive in many quarters.

Standards

Until the recent release of English Heritage's Draft Guidelines on Architectural Paint Research (See paper 9), it had been fourteen years since Frank Welsh, the American paint researcher, published his 'Call for Standards' in a North American preservation journal.[6]

In his article, Mr Welsh listed the minimum requirements of a paint analyst:

- Working knowledge and developed skills with stereo and polarized light microscopy and microchemical testing techniques, demonstrated through specific study and experience.
- Comprehension of architectural building history and technology, demonstrated through specific study and experience.
- Knowledge of historic architectural-finishes manufacture and application technology, as demonstrated through study, experience, teaching, lecturing, publishing, etc.
- True understanding and perception of color and how pigments and paint colors are affected by aging [sic].
- Professional willingness and ability to evaluate findings and/or techniques with others who are qualified in relation to individual project/client requirements.

These criteria have not changed, although they do need re-emphasizing.

Experience of researcher

A good paint researcher will probably have been doing the job for ten years or more; will have made some form of contribution to the field, and have carried out a hundred or so projects. In other words, he will be somebody who knows exactly what he is doing. The client should listen to the researcher, whose aim will be to carry out the job as quickly, accurately and efficiently as possible.

Projects take many forms. If advice is wanted on the way that colour was used in an interior of a particular period, a report should not take too long to prepare. However, if an analysis of the paint is required, it is essential that enough time to complete the work is allowed. Whilst it is possible that an interim report can be issued within a few weeks, a full, illustrated report – possibly amounting to 70 or more pages – will take much longer to produce. The size and complexity of the job will obviously have a direct bearing on this.

A client should not try to specify the number and location of samples to be taken. It is possible that repairs have been carried out previously, and sufficient samples need to be taken to avoid such anomalies. It is equally possible that surface detailing, or polychromatic decoration, was employed. It is far quicker for the researcher to take all the samples that are needed at one time, than to make an unnecessary return visit. A sketchy report will seldom justify the effort, and may well raise many unanswered questions.

Unrealistic expectations

On the matter of return visits, occasionally the researcher will need to go back to the site, in order to take confirmatory samples. Time must be allowed for this eventuality. To be told, as I was, that a project had to be completed as follows, defies belief. In this case the contract, following the tendering operation, was to be awarded on 4 February. Samples were to be removed by 18 February (some two weeks later), and the report was to be submitted by 3 March (i.e. within a month). Furthermore, access was limited to six hours on Sundays and Mondays, Wednesdays and Thursdays. Accommodation would be necessary, because of the distance from home, and the Tuesday would be spent inactive as the site was closed. This was not just for one room, but five areas of a building known to contain nineteenth-century polychromatic decoration.

As if to emphasize the ignorance of the project managers, the colours identified had to conform to RAL numbers, a range of colours standardized by the *Reichsausschuss für Lieferbedingungen* (RAL).[7] This organization was founded in Berlin, in 1925, to regulate and set the standards for quality in industry. Quite what would have happened if each of the colours did not match the 180 or so colours in that range was not explained. This business of specified paint colours will be discussed later.

'Cowboys'

As with any specialized, and little understood, discipline, there is no shortage of 'cowboys'. Certainly, there is every reason for a potential client to be hesitant about accepting the first quote for paint analysis. I was recently asked to look at a building where, before my arrival, the information revealed by a paint scrapist was found to be wanting. When asked to recommend somebody who could take and examine cross-sections, my client had been told that 600 samples would need to be taken from within the room, and that the bill would be in the region of £30,000. My quote was less than a tenth of that.

Clearly it is important to keep costs down to a minimum, but to try to handicap the analysis by limiting the samples to an unrealistically low number is self-defeating, and no researcher worthy of that name will comply with such a request. Analysis is not always warranted nor relevant in many instances. Provided that the original paint is not removed and no damage is caused by overpainting, the earlier layers can be left for analysis at some time in the future.

An inexperienced researcher may offer to take a few samples from a large number of rooms with the aim of helping the client form an idea of the general treatment. This can backfire if the client, or as happened to me on one particular project when an English Heritage inspector appeared on the scene and insisted on knowing how each moulding and element in 23 rooms had been treated. Three years later, I was still going backwards and forwards in order to answer increasingly specific questions. In spite of being allowed to put in a slightly larger bill for this extra work, it turned into another *pro bono* job.

The brief

The paint researcher will want to have a clear brief. Why is the project being carried out, and with what aim in mind? Just to ask for 'paint research' is not enough.

Is the first scheme applied to a surface considered the most important, or perhaps that was just an interim scheme applied before the full carbonation of the lime plaster? Fresh lime plaster has a high pH, and can adversely affect an oil paint that is applied directly on it. Traditionally a surface was allowed to dry out, and the pH levels to drop, before a scheme in oil paint was put on. A water-based soft distemper, which allowed a certain passage of moisture vapour, was often applied as an interim measure.

Perhaps an analysis of the first scheme, with a summary of the later 'significant' ones would be more useful? Schemes that are slightly unusual or noteworthy in some way, such as painted imitations of marble or woodgrain, might be included in such a summary. Information on the use of gilding, the presence of expensive pigments, or finishes that one might not expect to find on such a surface might also prove of interest.

Bear in mind that if one wants to know about the decoration applied during the occupancy of a notable individual, a full analysis may be required in order to establish datum points both before and after that period. The positive identification of pigments and components within many of the paint layers will be especially relevant in this sort of situation.

Inevitably, if a full-blown analysis is required, it will not be cheap. The report following such work may well go into great detail outlining the components and appearance of each of 30 or so schemes applied to a surface, and may involve, where appropriate, the use of some bought-in material analysis services such as scanning electron microscopy.

Appropriate information

Having said that, the mighty weight of detailed scientific analysis is sometimes misused, and the results are not altogether relevant. When investigating house paint a thorough understanding of the methods and materials of the early house-painter will often enable a clear interpretation of the paint stratigraphy seen under the microscope. The client should listen to the advice of the researcher on the type of analysis appropriate to answering his brief.

A few years ago I was asked to look at a couple of cross-sections in the laboratories of a major museum. The technicians knew that the paint from a late eighteenth-century room contained lead, phosphorous and possibly carbon, but were unsure what this indicated. They did not know whether it was unusual, nor what sort of colour would have been produced. No one in that laboratory had any background in architectural paint.

A few days later, following a lecture, I was asked what methods I employed for medium analysis. I looked rather blankly at my questioner, and said that beyond identifying whether a scheme was in oil or water, there was seldom a need to go further. It was clear that I had failed to convince him, but whether a house paint was based on raw linseed oil, boiled linseed oil, walnut oil, or poppy oil in most cases is not going to justify the expense required to find out.

Context, price and location would often suggest which oil was employed:

- Interior colours would generally be made up with raw linseed oil;
- An early exterior paint is likely to have contained boiled linseed oil;
- Being paler, walnut oil appears to have been widely used to obtain a white on large expanses;
- Poppy oil seems to have been used infrequently. It was the palest of the vegetable oils, and was rather expensive.

If it is considered important to establish paint media it is possible to commission such analysis.

Exterior railings, which date from the seventeenth and eighteenth century and have not been stripped invariably display a sequence of greys, greens, sometimes red-browns, and latterly black. To be asked, as I was a number of years ago, to determine the pigments and media used in all the decorative schemes applied to a set of railings dating from the 1860s made little sense. As a matter of course, I will usually indicate the presence of any date-relevant pigment, such as titanium dioxide (which tends to appear from the late 1920s onwards), and will certainly record the sequence of colours. However, quite what was achieved by having to report on the constituents of each of the schemes, including the undercoats was lost on me and, I suspect, the client.

Posing the question 'So what?' to the client at the outset of the project will generally prevent the production of a meaningless paint report. The information given should be presented so as to answer a clearly defined brief. What do the facts reported tell us about the building or structure? Do they answer the client's questions? Above all, the researcher must not lose sight of the fact that his report should be comprehensible and not full of obscure technical jargon.

I well remember going to look at a small terrace of derelict late eighteenth-century houses that were being renovated as part of a housing project scheme. Having walked around the buildings, I suggested that rather than employing paint analysis, the client should consider painting the buildings in a manner that reflected conventions of that period. However, I was persuaded to take samples from remnants of damaged skirting boards and from joinery that had been removed, poorly labelled, and put into store. The plaster had been hacked off in several rooms and my report was spectacularly unrevealing. Pretty well each paragraph would have failed the 'So what?' test.

Skills of the researcher

I have tried to emphasize the importance of appointing a paint researcher who knows their job. They will have experience of many technical and aesthetic aspects of decoration, paint, and colour, and will know how to combine theory with practice and be able to assist with the preparation of the schedule of redecoration. But remember, just because the researcher has a passing acquaintance with science does not mean that he will not know his Adam from his Yenn, nor his Asprucci from his Botticelli.

As well as understanding modern colour theory, the paint researcher will know of early notions of colour harmony; the effect created by combining various pigments; the colours available and popular in certain periods, and have a sound knowledge of early texts on house painting and decoration. He will also have seen the results of numerous redecoration projects. Furthermore he will be able to advise on the correct type and finish of paint to be used. To suggest that he is, almost by definition, somehow visually inept, and lacking in aesthetic sensibility, is likely to be far off the mark.

There is a common fallacy (and this is unlikely to endear me to the two professions): in matters of decoration, architects and architectural historians invariably know best. They may well be masters of their chosen fields, but are unlikely to have made a deep study of architectural colour.

Sharing of information

House curators are often reluctant to pass on the most basic of information that might help with the paint research. There is occasionally a tendency to regard the paint researcher as a member of one of the mechanical trades. It is frequently the case that copies of building accounts and other documentary information are not passed on, because it is not considered relevant to the project, almost as if there is a wide gulf between the historical research and paint analysis. Furthermore, the researcher is sometimes regarded as not the sort of person who might understand such documents. Even on one of the largest restoration projects carried out in the last ten years, a lot of persuasion was required before I was allowed sight of the allegedly unimportant family papers.

Do consider that a paint researcher, in many instances, can turn a seemingly bald entry in an account book into a colour; into a medium (i.e. oil or water), and also a finish (i.e. flat or glossy). The colour of the border boards in the Privy Garden, at Hampton Court, for example, was identified as a deep green by a knowledge of the price of painters' work and materials in the 1700s. Analysis of the paint was not possible as the original border boards had long since perished.

Frequently I have been told that there is no relevant documentary information, and almost as though it were an initiative test, have been left to learn of the history of the house from commonplace sources. After one particular job, I received a letter from the curator thanking me for 'the absolutely brilliant' comments on the paint, but then castigating me for not having referred to her latest version of the guidebook. Had I been supplied with the newest information on the house the relevant chapter in my report would have been up to date, and the interpretation of the cross-sections made somewhat easier.

The 'Doubting Thomas'

Exceptionally, one will come across a curator who refuses to believe what has been found, claiming that it counters accepted historic practice, but citing no evidence. The only occasion where this happened to me concerned a series of dark red-browns being identified on doors and skirting boards of an early eighteenth-century London house, which the curator refused to accept as being the early decorative finishes. It was suggested by the curator that the sequence of these early schemes with alternating varnish layers, were perhaps undercoats based on red lead, and not the red and brown oxides that had been identified by analysis, and illustrated by photomicrographs in the report. A careful letter, citing numerous documentary and pictorial examples to support the use of brown on doors and skirtings, eventually convinced the client of the accuracy of the analysis. However, one was left wondering whether that curator would not have been happier employing an interior designer to devise 'tasteful' schemes not so challenging to the preconceived ideas of the curator (Figure 4.1).

Health and safety issues

There is no doubt that a well-trained paint researcher will have wide-ranging skills, but a fearless, death-defying superman he is not.

Perhaps one of the most frequent problems encountered by the analyst is the failure of the client to provide safe, or even adequate, access. Even I, who used to be a military parachutist in a previous existence, find some of the ladders and scaffolds offered to me scary in the extreme. Indeed, there have been times when I have wondered if I would ever complete the sampling in one piece (Figure 4.2).

It is unrealistic, indeed it can only lead to heavily-qualified statements in the final report, to expect a whole ceiling to be sampled from an immovable platform. If elaborately decorated it is possible that 50 or more samples will need to be taken. Sometimes too, one is asked to examine a ceiling 40 or 50 feet high. It is immensely helpful, and reduces much time-wasting, if one can call on help to move the tower.

A researcher is only human and needs a few basic facilities in order to function efficiently. Sites are often cold, and a wise consultant will have learnt to bring adequate clothing, and a sandwich or two in order to survive the day's sampling. However, the provision of water and sanitation allows one to concentrate fully on the paint in a room, and prevents unnecessary anxiety, and lengthy interruptions while the local geography is explored.

Light too, comes in handy, if one is to make an effective examination. It really does help if the researcher is warned beforehand to make special arrangements if there is no power on site. However, in such an instance the client must not be surprised if the expenses part of the final bill is increased to reflect these arrangements. Is it realistic for a London-based analyst to arrange for scaffolding towers and lighting if the job is in Scotland? Surely the client will have far better local knowledge of how to arrange these things.

Colour references

Paint researchers are a hardy lot, and have, and will battle on against most impediments thrown in their way, but there is perhaps one thing that is guaranteed to cause them to question the seriousness of their client's intentions. This concerns a frequent insistence that the nearest British Standard, or RAL, colour reference is quoted for each of the colours encountered during analysis. This almost amounts to the same as Henry Ford's famous dictum 'The customer can have any colour he wants so long as it's black.'

On many occasions the researcher submits his report, and that is the end of his input. Often, years later, he may revisit the site and see a most hideous misinterpretation, something that could have been avoided by a continued, albeit small scale, involvement with the project.

An architectural paint research report is not a redecoration specification. However, if appropriate, a paint colour can be indicated in the report by a painted sample, and the relevant colorimetric information ought to be included in order that the paint can be reproduced exactly.

Spectrophotometry

Spectrophotometry has consigned paint ranges with only 57 varieties to the scrap heap, and now nearly every colour can be reproduced with a degree of accuracy hitherto unknown (Figure 4.3).

Not only can a paint be produced that matches that found on a site, but it is possible to ensure that each tin that is applied matches the standard (or target) exactly. Future maintenance implications should be considered. Surely it is better to formulate the required colour exactly, so that any quantity can be bought on a future occasion with no delay or unnecessary expense?

For a happy, successful, result it is essential that the client endeavours to work with the paint researcher and not against him. Use him for everything that he can offer. Often as a result of making the inevitable mistakes in his early years he has a great deal of practical experience to draw on.

References

1. Phillips, M. and Whitney, C., 'The Restoration of Original Paints at Otis House', *Old Time New England*, The Society for the Preservation of New England Antiquities, Vol LXII No 1, summer 1971, pp. 25–28.
2. Phillips, M., 'Problems in the Restoration and Preservation of Old House Paints', *Preservation and Conservation: Principles and Practices*, The Preservation Press, Washington D.C., 1972, pp. 273–285.
3. Bristow, I. C., 'Repainting Eighteenth-Century Interiors', *ASCHB Transactions*, Vol VI, 1982, pp. 25–33.
4. Baty, P., 'The Role of Paint Analysis in the Historic Interior', *Journal of Architectural Conservation*, Vol 1 No1, March 1995, pp. 27–37.
5. Baty, P., 'To Scrape or Not', *Traditional Paint News*, Vol 1, No 2, October 1996, pp. 4–5.
6. Welsh, F., 'Call for Standards', *Association for Preservation Technology Bulletin*, Vol XVIII, No 4, 1986, pp. 4–5.
7. National Board of Supply Conditions, *Reichsausschuss für Lieferbedingungen* (RAL).

Architectural Paint Research in Practice

Ian Jardin

The Major Projects Department of English Heritage was set up in 1995 specifically to handle discrete projects that would overstretch the day-to-day capacity of the rest of the organization. It enabled English Heritage to tackle large, problematic or risky building projects, in particular it made possible direct intervention in otherwise insoluble Building at Risk cases, where indirect English Heritage involvement in the form of grant-aid and advice to owners did not work. Danson House, which I shall discuss further, was an early classic example of this.

As a project director in Major Projects, I was asked to present this paper because our work may give some idea of the client's view of architectural paint research. As a department we represent the interest of the building's owner, in this case English Heritage. We do not carry out the work ourselves but we procure it on behalf of the owner, commissioning external consultants and contractors and also internal consultants, i.e. English Heritage staff, who work side by side with external project members on the job.

In looking at English Heritage as a client, I would however issue one health warning. Our very purpose is to conserve historic buildings and increase public understanding and enjoyment of them; we are therefore predisposed to paint research and any other kind of building research. The same may not be true of private clients who have functional needs for their buildings and other demands on their money. There is a big difference between such clients and public or charitable bodies such as English Heritage and The National Trust, whose purpose is to care for historic buildings.

Paint research has been an element of almost every English Heritage major project so far. Examples of this include Darwin's home at Down House, Eltham Palace, Bolsover Castle, Kenwood House, Rangers House and several others. But I would like to focus on one project in particular, the library in Danson House.

Danson House is a Palladian villa built in the 1760s to the designs of Sir Robert Taylor for a City merchant, Sir John Boyd. The heart of the house is a *piano nobile* consisting of four grand rooms around a central top-lit stairwell. Danson is listed Grade I reflecting the building's status as a superb piece of architecture both inside and out (Figure 5.1).

By the early 1990s it was one of the most notorious and long-standing Building at Risk cases in the country. The Danson estate, and with it the house, was bought by the local council in the 1920s for use as a public park, and thereafter the house received very little appropriate maintenance. This exacerbated structural problems caused by earlier alterations, and by the 1970s the building was in an advanced state of deterioration, riddled by dry rot. In the 1980s the situation was exacerbated by a tenant who was taken on by the council to repair the building, but instead stripped out much of its plasterwork tracing dry rot, and removed a substantial amount of the joinery and other fittings to pay off business debts. Fortunately these were later recovered. By 1995, when English Heritage intervened directly and acquired the building from the local council, the state of the interiors presented a challenge in terms of repair and presentation.

As a result of this context of neglect, English Heritage was presented with a radically damaged building with much of its internal fabric missing. In each of the principal rooms much of the original fabric was completely lost, but equally much survived. At this point, unless the building was merely to be structurally stabilized and maintained as a ruin, any repair of the internal fabric would be, at least in part, a restoration. At the same time there was much fabric left, to which, on the face of it, our usual 'conserve as found' philosophy could be applied. But at this stage, the extent of our historical knowledge of the building and our detailed understanding of the fabric which would be needed to work out whatever restoration or conservation work could be carried out in detail, was limited.

This is where building research in all its forms – including paint research, archaeological research, historical research and our architects and engineers analysis of the structure – played such an important part. Initially our assumption was that we would be conserving as found, and that the aim of this research and analysis was, in effect, to match the restoration of the lost fabric to conservation of what survived *in situ*. But as our research team came to understand more and more about the building, we all came to realise that this obvious option was not necessarily the only or even the best one.

From a combination of all the research, it became clear that the history of the building's materials was not one of gradual changes, difficult to unravel; rather that the principal rooms had been almost unchanged for the first 100 years of Danson's existence, apart from some minor works. A new owner in the 1860s carried out a major refurbishment. His additions consisted mainly of overlaid fittings, such as gas lighting, and applied papier-mâché mouldings, rather than destructive alterations to the Georgian features. Following the 1860s refurbishment there were again no further major changes until the structural degradations of the twentieth century. It thus became clear that the original Georgian rooms survived beneath the literally superficial Victorian additions.

This created a conundrum. The condition that the building was found in was effectively that of the 1860s refurbishment, but the presentation of the interiors in this form would still be in part a restoration, and a very expensive one at that, since many of the Victorian fittings were themselves lost and destroyed with the rooms. On the other hand we now knew, thanks to the research, that the original 1760s rooms could be reinstated in the course of repair and could be confidently presented as such.

The decision was therefore made to restore the original 1760s interior. The purpose of this paper is not to discuss or explain the background to this decision, but rather to use it as an example of how paint research played an important part in this major project. In order to illustrate this in detail I will examine the Library.

The east wall of the Library consists of a centrally positioned chimneypiece flanked by bookcases, which in turn are flanked by doors connected to the adjoining rooms. When we took over the house two elliptical plaster plaques survived *in situ* above the doors. The central wall position above the chimneypiece was blank but there was the obvious evidence from a paint shadow that a large painting had previously hung there – confirmed by archive photographs).

Meanwhile in the side passage off the Entrance Hall there was a larger round plaque, stylistically similar to the smaller plaques surviving in the Library (Figure 5.2). The position of this plaque in the service space could not conceivably have been its original one. The obvious possibility was that it originated from the Library along with the similar pair and the most obvious place for it was above the chimneypiece. But however obvious the possibility, it was still speculation. There was no hard evidence to justify the restoration of the plaque to a new position. This hard evidence was supplied by paint research, in combination with the other key research disciplines, which are listed below.

Structural archaeological evidence

Cutting through a section of plaster above the chimneypiece revealed a circular hole in the original plaster and underlying laths and battens. This was filled in with further lath and plasterwork, presumably at a later date. The dimensions of this feature were exactly 1050 mm in diameter; the measurement of the displaced round plaque, with some allowance for a lost edge moulding, showed that it was just a fraction under 1050 mm in diameter. This evidence was nearly, but not yet completely, convincing.

The historian's evidence

Archival research revealed a number of other mid-Georgian buildings containing identical copies of both the large round and the smaller elliptical plaques, although not necessarily together in one building, let alone in one room. However, comparative evidence for the placement of the three plaques was found in the Dining Room at The Oaks, Carshalton, another Taylor building which was demolished in the late 1950s. A surviving photograph shows identical versions of both the large round plaque and the smaller elliptical plaques in combination on one wall. This provides strong historical evidence, but is still not completely convincing evidence for the existence of such an arrangement in the Library at Danson.

Paint research

Sampling of the displaced round plaque revealed three layers of white paint, representing one original scheme plus two interim repainting redecorations (Figure 5.3). These were identical to the earliest paint layers found on the *in situ* elliptical plaques; however the round plaque lacked the five later layers of green and blue paint found on the elliptical plaques (Figure 5.4). When samples of the infill plaster from the circular scar above the chimneypiece were compared with samples of the surrounding untouched wall plaster, it was found that this infill plaster carried the later layers, but lacked the earliest paint layer found on the surrounding wall (Figure 5.5). Based on this evidence we can be certain that the displaced plaque was indeed originally above the Library chimneypiece and that it was removed before the Library was redecorated in the nineteenth century. In confirmation of this, traces of the earliest paint layers on the Library walls were found on the edges of the displaced plaque.

The evidence from the architectural paint research confirmed our suspicions and we were then able to confidently remove the round plaque from the passage and reinstate it in its original position over the chimneypiece (Figures 5.6, 5.7 and 5.8).

I would like to emphasize that this small example of the work carried out at Danson does not explain the sheer sophistication of what was being done by our team. This calibre of research was repeated across the building and gave us the necessary information to support the case for returning the interiors to their original 1760s form. Without this solid support from a team of conservation professionals we could not have expected to gain either approval for the project from English Heritage's own Historic Buildings Advisory Committee or Listed Building Consent.

Conclusions

I would suggest that paint research is not just about identifying authentic historic paint schemes. Fascinating and valuable though this is, paint research forms a very powerful part of buildings' archaeology. Archaeology, whether it is concerned with the analysis of standing buildings or the excavation of buried features, is in good part about identifying and interpreting strata. One of the media in which strata survive in buildings is, of course, the paint layer. I would also add a health warning here. Such research should not be an excuse for every owner to attempt a restoration such as this. At Danson there was no other option than to restore the building once the notion of preserving the structure as a ruin had been dismissed. The same circumstances cannot be applied to other buildings indiscriminately.

Further I would conclude that to be effective, paint researchers must form part of a wider research team. They must intuitively be team players and they must be willing to share their results with other specialists to develop ideas collectively. They must be able to sublimate their professional personalities within the whole. I realise that such an approach can go very much against the grain of academic research where exclusive discovery is of such importance. With that said, I acknowledge that clients and managers for their part must always ensure that individuals get due recognition, and not least because professionals will not be able to build up viable business without some recognition.

At Danson we were lucky enough to have as good a team as you can get, and a team that most certainly did work freely and well together. I take every opportunity to mention them and thank them because they were superb. The team consisted of: Richard Lee of English Heritage's Historical Analysis Research Team, Chris Miele, formerly of the same English Heritage team and now with Alan Baxter Associates, Jamie Coath a conservation architect with Purcell Miller Tritton; and Helen Hughes, English Heritage's Senior Paint Researcher.

Our team's skills stood out because they are so rare. It is relatively easy for English Heritage to secure the best in the field for exceptional projects such as Danson, but there are many more buildings that would benefit from their skills. If paint research and its allied disciplines are to prosper then the likes of Helen, Chris, Jamie and Richard must therefore be bred or cloned.

Paint and other research must be built into a project from the very beginning, with sufficient time and money being allowed for it. Moreover, the client must programme in sufficient time to allow the research team to pool and develop their thoughts. It may, therefore, come as some surprise when I say that I believe researcher's briefs on projects similar to Danson should be kept flexible. This is provided that there is a reasonable contingency provision to keep things under some control and provided that the contractual arrangements allow the researcher proper, but not uncontrolled, recompense. It also follows that the project should be programmed to allow for quite radical changes of direction if this is what the research indicates.

I fear that this approach goes against the grain of professional project management. But it is important that clients and managers understand and respect the disciplines they are working with and do not unintentionally 'throw the baby out with the bath water'.

There is of course a counterpart to this: researchers for their part must appreciate the needs and the pressures of clients and their managers. Building is the most expensive and risky activity most of us can ever engage in. However important the building there must be a budget, a programme and a tight definition and structure of work. Un-programmed delays can cost a great deal of money, and research that arrives too late is useless for the conservation of the building (whatever it does for the academic reputation of the researcher). Researchers understand and respect this. They must be businesslike; they must appreciate the needs of builders they may work alongside; they must understand contracts and they must read the small print. For example if they have contracted to perform a task within a given time and cost, they must do it. If they do not then it is likely there will be one less client for paint research in the future, and that would be very sad.

I think research should be a recognized phase in building projects, certainly in large projects such as Danson. Research should certainly be carried out by appointed professionals at an early stage in a project, in much the same way we appoint architects to survey the building. It should perhaps be carried out as part of the Conservation Plan. Conservation plans are meant to establish as much what you don't know about a particular site as what you do know, creating a marker for later research. But in the case of bodies such as English Heritage perhaps there should also be the opportunity to carry out research before we even start the project.

I confess that in early projects such as Danson, we did not ourselves deploy research as well as we might have done. Our team was put together gradually, with some false starts on the paint research side, and our initial definition of the project could have been better. But I hope that we were flexible in allowing effective and very fruitful research to emerge, to the ultimate benefit of the building and of the public who will enjoy it. It is essential not to forget this positive aspect about research for public or private clients: it tells you so much. Since the initial work at Danson was finished we have occasionally been able to take members of the public around the building, and they find it fascinating. People want to know more. There is a hunger among the general public to know more about this sort of thing – which is tremendous for owners such as us.

I believe that the success of Danson was aided by me, as the client, having some knowledge of what paint research is and what it can provide, based in no small part on the teachings of Ian Bristow. The same cannot be said of all clients, nor even of all conservation practitioners, even within English Heritage. So if I have one last message it is this: 'go forth and educate'.

Architectural Paint Research: The Dutch Experience and Perspective

Angelique Friedrichs

I would like to outline the architectural paint research training that is provided by the Stichting Restauratie Atelier Limburg, as part of the Decorative Historic Interiors Conservation Course, with reference to two case studies. In each of these projects the paint research was of great importance. I will also mention the status of architectural paint research and plans concerning the future development of this subject in The Netherlands. However, I want to start with explaining the background and philosophy of the course.

The Decorative Interior Conservation Course, Maastricht

The Stichting Restauratie Atelier Limburg is a provincial conservation studio that since 1990 has provided a five-year postgraduate training programme in conservation of paintings and painted objects. The course is divided between a three-year period in the Maastricht studios and two years of internships in museums and heritage organizations in The Netherlands and abroad. It focuses on three conservation disciplines: old master paintings, modern art and decorative historic interiors.

Seven years ago our director, Anne van Grevenstein, felt the need to call attention to the conservation of the historic interior. Compared to works of art conserved in a museum context, decorative schemes in interiors did not get sufficient attention in The Netherlands. The conservators employed frequently lacked the detailed knowledge which the treatment of decorative surfaces requires. Besides, when an interior contains for example canvas paintings attached to the wall, a painted plaster ceiling, and painted wooden panelling, the conservation and restoration of each element is usually executed by a variety of specialists. Decorators and carpenters as well as conservators are also involved. The paintings' conservator may remove the canvas paintings from the room for treatment in his studio where he may decide not to remove all the varnish, but leave a thin layer of patina. The conservator of the painted ceiling, on the other hand, may use a cleaning agent that removes every speck of ingrained dirt, and the architect makes some quick paint scrapes on the panelling to define the 'original' colour scheme. There is no exchange of information, no co-operation and no unity in the philosophy of the treatment. I have not even mentioned the sometimes very intrusive work of the building contractor, the plumber or the electrician. Maybe this is an exaggerated representation, but unfortunately this situation is still common practice in a lot of historic buildings in The Netherlands. Conservation campaigns in historic interiors can be complex and unpredictable. Ensuring that different professions work in unison, through co-operation and communication can be laborious, difficult and often impossible.

The main goal of the Decorative Historic Interior course offered at Maastricht is to train conservators who have a broad overview of all the different problems they encounter when working in an interior. Apart from a compressed programme dealing with the more general issues of paintings' conservation, which is taught jointly with the students of the other two courses, the historic interior students learn about specific aspects pertaining to the conservation of interiors. Attention is paid to historical and technical aspects of wallpaper, gilded leather, ornamental stucco, wall-linings, architectural paint research, decorative painting techniques (graining, marbling, gilding, lacquerwork) and decorations on wainscoting and plaster. Topics such as environmental control and structural aspects of building conservation require special consideration. From day one, the students on the course gain practical experience by working with staff members on site where they are actively involved in assessing research requests, devising treatment proposals and estimating costs. Consultation with architects, painters, contractors or other conservators is also seen as an important part of their training. The course includes a broad range of subjects and problems. The students are made aware of the fact that as each conservation field is very specific and specialized, it will always be necessary to liaise with other specialist conservators or recommend the use of their services.

Historic interiors are altered by their history of use and owners. Before a conservation campaign can begin, one has to unravel this history and a structural examination always forms a significant part of the conservation of an interior. It is necessary to understand the meaning, background, dates and even more crucially, the relationships of all the components of the interior. Architectural paint research offers a useful tool for the disclosure of the history of a building. The examination of the build-up of paint layers on panelling and the pigments used can give incontrovertible evidence about the date or relative age of elements.

Case study – an eighteenth-century Grand Drawing Room, Houthem-St.Gerlach

One of our early projects was the conservation of some late nineteenth-century interiors in an early eighteenth-century house in Houthem-St.Gerlach, a small village not far from Maastricht. The Project team included Anne van Grevenstein, Ruth Jongsma, Jos van Och, Josefien Tegelaar, Edwin Verweij, Nico van der Wouden, and myself.

The Grand Drawing Room contained painted canvas wall linings, decorated panelling, a painted ceiling and ornate plaster mouldings (Figure 6.1). Research revealed that not much had changed in this room since its nineteenth-century refitting. An extensive architectural paint research strategy was not necessary because the panelling retained the original black and gold scheme. In the cove of the ceiling is written *'dezen blavong is gemaakt in Den Mei 1879 door Johan Josepf Köhlen'* (this ceiling was made in May 1879 by Johan Josepf Köhlen) and at the back of one of the painted canvas wall linings: *'finit le 1. Aout 1872'* (finished 1st August 1872). The ceiling still contains its late nineteenth-century painted flower tendrils and the wall-linings are neatly fitted in frames bearing paint layers comparable to those found on the panelling. Only the chimneypiece dates from the eighteenth century.

The soft orange coloured paintings with neo-classical decorations were painted on a finely textured canvas. These canvases were glued on sheets of paper, and then glued onto a coarsely woven canvas. Because the size of the paintings is smaller than the space of the wall to be decorated, the coarse canvasses were larger than the paintings. These canvasses were attached to the wooden structure and fitted to the wall. The frames surrounding the paintings are placed on top of this whole structure. The exposed areas of the coarse backing canvases were originally painted in the same soft orange colour as the paintings but at some date these areas had obviously been overpainted in a dark brown paint.

The coarse backing canvas had deteriorated considerably in time: there were tears and holes in many places and the adhesion between the paintings and the backing canvas was poor. The thick brown overpaint had curled and flaked in big pieces, deforming the canvas.

It was necessary to remove the coarse backing canvas from the paintings and attach a new lining canvas. After this treatment a soft orange-coloured paint was applied to the new canvas visible around the edge of the paintings. The result was surprizing; all the pieces of the interior were coming together again, the proportions of the room were better balanced and the colours more harmonious. The colour change had a great impact on the architectural space. This project made it clear how important it is to incorporate all elements of an interior and that architectural paint research should not be strictly limited to the architectural elements (Figure 6.2).

Case study – a Nineteenth-century reception room, Kockengen, Utrecht

The reception room in a house in Kockengen, a small village near Utrecht, is decorated with panoramic landscapes (Figure 6.3). The following people were also involved in this research and conservation project, Bernice Crijns, Helene Dubois, Elsbeth Geldhof, Danielle van Kempen, Katherine Kolff, Jos van Och, and Martijn Terhorst. At the time of our first visit to the house to make an initial inspection of the large paintings, a firm of housepainters were decorating the adjacent hall. The owners of the house planned to paint the panelling of the reception room immediately after the hall was finished. Fearing that our treatment of large canvases might inadvertently scuff or dirty any newly painted panelling in the room, we managed to convince the owners to postpone the redecoration of the reception room until we had completed our work. We also suggested that it might be interesting to search for traces of old paint layers and attempt to establish the original colour of the joinery at the time when the panoramic landscapes were introduced. Thus, an examination of the architectural paint was instigated.

The panoramic paintings are the most important and eye catching element of this interior. For this reason we choose to identify the paint scheme that had been applied to the panelling in 1802 when the landscapes, painted by the Utrecht artist Hendrick van Barneveldt, were installed in the room. Paint scrapes carried out on the oldest elements of the panelling revealed a grey-green background applied over a pinkish-white ground as the first scheme. Examination in cross-section of this grey-green layer revealed that it contained a mixture of lead white and a black pigment. The pinkish-white ground was composed of lead white tinted with some brown and red particles. On a quarter round moulding of a ceiling beam, an additional green layer was found on top of the grey-green layer; which in cross-section was shown to be a mixture of white tinted with yellow and fine blue pigment particles. This same green layer was also found on a vertical wooden post next to the door. As part of the structural repairs to the joinery, it was necessary to remove a moulded fillet from the top of the dado rail. This fillet had protected a fragment of the original grey-green background, embellished with a green horizontal border and dark green dots with yellow highlights (Figure 6.4). The pigment composition of the dark green dots was analysed by The Netherlands Institute for Cultural Heritage. The green colour contained lead white, Naples yellow, Prussian blue and some chalk (Figure 6.5).[1]

Because the date of the oldest elements (for example the posts on either side of the doors and the ceiling) is not known, it was uncertain whether the first paint layers were applied at the same time as the panoramic paintings. There was a possibility that the room had been in use for some time before the landscapes were installed; in which case the joinery might have been repainted when the paintings were first introduced. For this reason it was necessary to look for links between the decorations on both interior elements. As part of the conservation of a painted winter landscape above the door, it was necessary to remove the frame from around this painting. Underneath this frame a partly overpainted original green border was found on top of the painting. The colour of this border showed a distinct resemblance to the green colour found on the quarter-round moulding of the ceiling beam and the horizontal border and dots on the wooden post next to the door. Indeed, the cross-sections revealed the same pigment composition, albeit that the green paint layer overlapping the painting contained less chalk and more Prussian blue than that on the ceiling. The use of Naples yellow and Prussian blue to make a green colour was common practice in the eighteenth century. Although Naples yellow is found sporadically in panel paintings of the sixteenth century, it was not until the 1770s that it was commercially available and used for house-painting. By the 1780s Naples yellow was already being replaced by patent yellow, a cheaper and more durable pigment. Both yellow pigments were superceded in the 1820s by chrome yellow.[2] It is therefore plausible that the dark green colour on the panelling and the wall-linings could have been applied shortly after the completion of the landscapes in 1802. During the conservation treatment of the canvas paintings a few other green borders were discovered underneath some cover battens and later black overpaint. Unfortunately, as the horizontal posts on either side of the door are the only surviving original parts of the dado, we can only guess the appearance of this presumably very richly decorated room in c.1802. Further details of the research and treatment of this room in the house in Kockengen are outlined in Bulletin KNOB.[3]

Conclusion

These two case studies have shown the value of incorporating all the elements of an interior when conducting research into the history of a room. A deteriorated backing canvas with ugly curled brown paint, like that found in Houthem-St.Gerlach, might easily have been thrown away by a paintings' conservator; and in that case the architect would have chosen an arbitrary colour to apply to the canvas strips next to the paintings. Similarly in Kockengen it was fortunate that those responsible for the architectural paint research were also involved in the treatment of the landscape paintings. Here a clear link between the decoration of the panelling and the paintings could be established, providing a tantalizing glimpse of a very richly decorated room of c.1802.

So far I have not discussed the way the paint schemes in the interiors in Houthem-St.Gerlach and Kockengen were reconstructed. In The Netherlands there is hardly any experience in reconstructing paint schemes using traditional lead based linseed oil paints and on this subject we look with interest to what is happening in England. We can only benefit from your experience and research. Of course Ian Bristow's books contain a wealth of information.

Another reason for not using lead based linseed oil paints is that it is very difficult to persuade architects, owners and housepainters to use a paint system that they are not familiar with. Lead paint is a hazardous material and housepainters are cautious about using it. To develop our own knowledge and experience of traditional materials the students have painted out samples of old and modern paint systems on small panels and carefully noted the composition, the handling properties and visual appearance of the different systems (Figure 6.6). By conducting these trials we hope to be able to compare the visual properties of these paints ourselves and use them as tools to demonstrate to housepainters and houseowners the advantages of using traditional paint systems.

We have established links with a housepainter who is willing to experiment with traditional paint systems. It is very important to have someone who is open to suggestions and willing to cope with the fact that these systems are difficult to handle and also has the patience to mix a colour over and over again until its hue is just right.

Some of the former students of the course on decorative historic interiors now work as independent architectural paint researchers. Architectural paint research in The Netherlands is slowly gaining the interest of conservators, architects, building historians and others working for architectural heritage organizations. The knowledge of the history of painting techniques and architectural colours is still sparse in The Netherlands and so there are plans to develop a database to encourage the exchange of information and knowledge. Setting standards for architectural paint research is a first step to guaranteeing quality in this field; for this reason we are very interested in the *Layers of Understanding* seminar.

References

1 Pigment analysis was carried out by DeKeijer and Mensch for the Netherlandish Institute for Cultural Heritage, unpublished report 1999.
2 Bristow, I. C., *Interior House-painting Colours and Technology 1615–1840*, Yale University Press, New Haven and London, 1996, p. 36.
3 Bulletin KNOB (Koninklije Nederlandse Oudheidkundidge Bond, translates as Royal Netherlands Historical Heritage), Summer 2000.

Figure 6.1 The Grand Drawing Room in an early eighteenth-century house in Houthem-St. Gerlach, before treatment.
See paper 6

Figure 6.2 The Grand Drawing Room of the early eighteenth-century house illustrated in Figure 6.1 after treatment.
See paper 6

Figure 6.3 The Reception Room in a house in Kockengen, showing the painted panoramic landscapes of 1802, before treatment. **See paper 6**

Figure 6.4 Fragment of the original grey-green scheme on a vertical wooden post next to the door in the Reception Room in Kockengen. The small area had been overpainted in the past. **See paper 6**

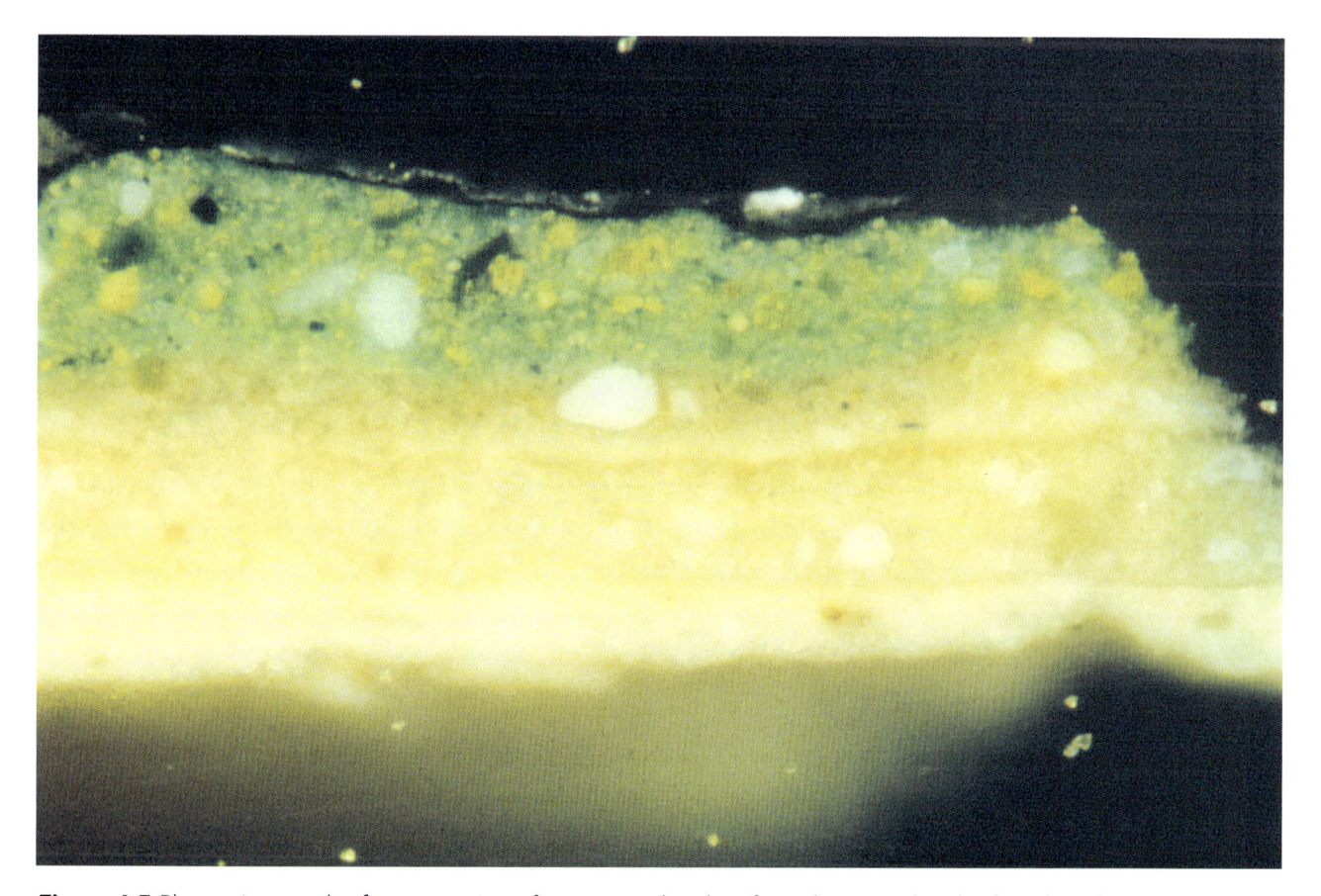

Figure 6.5 Photomicrograph of cross-section of paint sample taken from the green border found on the vertical wooden post illustrated in Figure 6.4, x 250 magnification. **See paper 6**

Figure 6.6 Lead paint trials being carried out by students from the Conservation Course on Decorative Historic Interiors in Maastricht.

See paper 6

Figure 8.1 The Library, Nostell Priory.
©The National Trust

See paper 8

Session 3

Statutory Requirements: Listed Building Requirements and PPG 15

James Edgar

Conservation practice covers a diverse range of building types and functions, but the vast majority of Listed Building Consent casework relates to public buildings such as museums. There are 4,000 Grade II listed buildings in Islington alone. Is architectural paint research and its surrounding issues really relevant to every one of these buildings?

It gives me cause for concern that there are only six or maybe ten local authority conservation officers on the delegate list. Conservation officers form a major constituent part of the people we should be educating, as they are the administrators at the forefront of the system which controls alterations to listed buildings.

In the course of this paper I intend to consider two questions which are of great significance for both the client and the conservation professional when considering changes to listed buildings in the context of architectural paint research:

- Is permission required for alterations to the decorative schemes of interiors of historic buildings?
- Does stripping require Listed Building Consent?

If the answer to these questions is 'yes' then what are the parameters and the guidance for decision makers, local authority conservation officers, English Heritage inspectorial staff and the Secretary of State?

My discussion of this issue adheres strictly to planning policy guidance as laid out in PPG 15.[1] This document, introduced in September 1994, contains the Government's policy guidance on all matters (except archaeology), relating to the historic environment; this includes paint research and analysis as well as the redecoration of historic interiors. This document, providing the first substantive guidance on interior paintwork and decoration, was introduced very late in the history of United Kingdom conservation.

Before 1994, central government guidance on the treatment of historic interiors was contained in one paragraph only, and this primarily related to the painting of facades. The only reference to the interiors related to decorated ceilings and concentrated on the plasterwork rather than the painted decoration.

Listed buildings are defined by the Government as buildings with special architectural and historic interest. As such they are included on the list compiled as a duty by the Secretary of State for Culture, Media and Sport. In 1994 the estimate in PPG 15 was that there are approximately 443,000 entries, but perhaps about 500,000 individual listed buildings.

How many of those 500,000 have important interiors? This is a question that we simply cannot answer. Excluding churches, there may be 400,000 listed buildings in England alone. I would like to have told you how many of them have decorative interiors of any type, but a search of our computerized listed building database has not provided the definitive answer. The search on interiors with decorative painting produced the staggeringly high figure of 8–9,000 Grade I and Grade II* buildings alone. But I would suggest that a vast majority of these entries relate to wall paintings in medieval houses.

I suspect that there may not be many, perhaps no more than a handful of historic buildings where decorative paintwork, as opposed to paintings, is visible and officially recognized as significant.

It has been suggested that the survival of any pre-1950 scheme would be unusual. It can also be confidently stated that most buildings of all periods, unless they have been deliberately stripped, will retain evidence of earlier decorative schemes. The first comment may be seen as relating to intact decorative schemes, the second to the archaeological evidence. In both cases we simply do not know the figures involved.

Having defined the relevant Government legislation and the current level of knowledge regarding the number of listed buildings to which this legislation pertains, I will return to our two important questions.

Is Listed Building Consent required to alter interiors?

The answer would appear to be straight-forward; PPG 15 says that once a building is listed consent is normally required for any works or alterations which would affect its character as a building of special architectural and historic interest. The emphasis is placed upon any works or alteration which would affect a building's 'character'. Consideration of whether any redecoration works would affect a building's character is essential for judging whether Listed Building Consent is needed. PPG 15 specifically mentions that where painting or repainting the exterior or interior of the listed building would affect the building's character, consent is required.

A review of the planning journals and appeal decisions for any case law or precedents was not very helpful. There are a number of published cases on the painting of exteriors, and this matter was finally settled in 1988. The judge in question actually said that in this case the critical test would be whether the repainting affected the character of the building as of special architectural and historic interest. He went on to say that little imagination was required to identify cases where repainting in unsuitable colours or using unsuitable renders would produce an unfortunate aesthetic result. He ended by saying he did not think that parliament could have intended such activities to be immune from listed building control. Does this also apply to interiors as well? The answer is yes, if the proposed alterations affect the character of the building. It is this case which generated a government circular in 1988. However, I could not find a single appeal or case law decision which has any direct relevance to our subject.

Is permission required? Yes, if the alteration affects the character of the building as a building of special architectural and historic interest. We are almost back to square one, the critical judgement to be made on a case by case basis by local planning authorities, remains that the character must be affected before consent is required, and the control mechanisms kick in. Critically, no guidance is provided on how to make that decision. It is worth noting that local planning authorities are not well represented at the *Layers of Understanding* seminar.

Let me quote the advice of an eminent planning and conservation barrister:[2]

In practice, common sense will usually supply the answer. Consent will only very exceptionally be needed for example for very minor works, such as rewiring or redecorating. But it should not be forgotten that sincerely held views on such matters can differ strongly. If in any doubt, anyone contemplating any works to listed building of any grade should seek advice from the planning authority or just submit an application.

Drawing on my own experience and information gathered from my colleagues, I have to say unequivocally that the number of cases I deal with where the redecoration of interiors is actually part of an application, never mind an application alone, is extremely low. In the last year, covering three counties, I have been involved in two such cases. One of them concerned pre-application discussion at Kelmarsh Hall, Northamptonshire and another a redundant church in Leicestershire. It cannot be argued that that is a reflection of rural poverty; during the years when I was dealing with central London cases, the number per annum cannot have been much higher. That has to be seen in the context of the City of Westminster where there are well over a thousand Listed Building Consent applications each year.

Interestingly, almost all of these were cases whose interiors were of a public rather than a private character. I can think of only one exceptional case where a private house comes to mind. These public buildings are often galleries or museums: the National Gallery, the National Portrait Gallery, the Royal Academy, the Courtauld Institute at Somerset House, and other museum character properties such as Robert Adam's Home House at Portland Place. My colleagues offered similar cases: Kenwood House, Bolsover Castle, Danson House, all English Heritage properties.

Does stripping require Listed Building Consent?

Returning to PPG 15, I will now consider the second question: how do the decision makers act? Can the decision makers ask for or demand sufficient information to enable them to make informed decisions on paintwork? Should the owners of the historic building applying for Listed Building Consent provide the local planning authority with full information to enable them to assess the likely impact of the proposals on the special architectural and historical interest of the building? My experience is that sometimes you are lucky if you get a 'before' and 'after' plan drawn by an architect, never mind anything so rarely found as paint analysis or a building research scheme. That is the harsh reality of the situation which is much worse in the rest of the country than it is in the City of Westminster.

PPG 15 tackles this question in the main body of the text, paragraph 3.12:

In judging the effect of any alteration or extension it is essential to have addressed the elements that make up the special interest of the building in question. They may comprise not only obvious visual features such as a decorative façade or, internally, staircases or decorated plaster ceilings, but the spaces and layout of the building and the archaeological or technological interest of the surviving structure and surfaces.

So there is some comfort there that we can take from the information provided by the Government. But the reality is that such assessments of buildings do not actually happen very often.

If the relevant assessment of the interior decoration has been carried out the annex at the back of PPG 15 provides further guidance. Information about the history and development of the building can be gained from the physical evidence of the building, from paint analysis as well as documentary information. It is also important to note when approaching any proposed redecoration that subsequent alterations include later decorative schemes. These do not necessarily detract from the character and interest of the building. Later features should not be removed merely to restore the building to an early form.

And the final general point of advice; the wholesale reinstatement of lost, destroyed or superseded elements of the building or an interior is not appropriate, although where a building has largely retained the integrity of its design, the reinstatement of lost or destroyed elements of that design could be considered.

The most important element of PPG 15 for redecoration is paragraph C63:

Interior paint work and decoration: A careful choice of both type and colour of paints or wallpapers can make a significant contribution to the appearance and integrity of a historic interior. Inappropriate schemes may, conversely, be visually damaging.

I believe that this provides me with sufficient authority to be able to say, if you want to paint an interior of a certain date, which probably should have been creamy stone colour, bright orange then you need Listed Building Consent, but you are not going to get it.

Paragraph C63 further states that:

In some instances specialist advice should be sought on the original scheme of decoration which may survive beneath later layers.

This advice is somewhat ambiguously termed, 'In some instances' doesn't indicate how many, or in which cases such advice should be sought, and certainly does not say how to go about gaining such guidance. This ambiguity is further compounded by paragraph C63:

Although strict adherence to historical forms is not normally a requirement in buildings whose interiors are of a 'private' rather than a 'museum' character, the use of historically appropriate decoration can greatly enhance most listed buildings.

The phrasing of this passage can be interpreted in a rather permissive way, seeming to allow a broad interpretation by the owner.

The paragraph closes with two important sentences:

Where important early schemes of interior decoration survive, cleaning and conservation rather than the renewal may be appropriate. Over painting, even of deteriorated or discoloured areas of plain colour may damage or obscure the historical record.

This suggests that an assessment of the existing scheme is required before redecoration is undertaken.

Conclusions

I would like to offer some thoughts and observations. We cannot depart from the fundamental test: would proposed alterations affect the character of a building with special architectural and historic interest? I suggest we need to consider this in the context of the following framework. In the context of extant paintwork, and by that I mean schemes that are visible, if the paint scheme is of historic interest, original or later, the presumption is in favour of its preservation. Conversely it would seem to be difficult to justify the retention of old plain paintwork as a working surface except where it has incontestable aesthetic or technological significance.

In the context of works schemes, further advice is desperately needed on how to recognize historic paint, and on a number of related topics. Is it now possible to paper or paint harmlessly over surfaces believed to be of some interest, but not well enough preserved to be displayed? It does occur to me that on this topic it would be helpful to have a definitive view on whether or not archaeological paint evidence can be accepted as contributing to the special interest of the character of the building. Do hidden fragmentary schemes of paintwork form part of the character of the building which make it worthy of listed status? In order to answer this question a case must be tested in the courts, and it would be a brave local authority who would go down that line in many cases.

Guidance is needed on where it is desirable or necessary to remove paintwork, for example if the underlying cornice detail is completely lost by layers and layers of overpainting, or where damp penetration makes it a physical necessity to remove paint. Guidance is needed on how to tackle such situations, including a best practice guide on how to remove, record, analyse and retain samples preferably *in situ*. Such archiving and research is essential in order to satisfy the archaeological aspects of the retention of historic paintwork.

Finally, in the context of new schemes in historic interiors, it is not possible to insist on the recreation of historic decorative schemes through the listed building consent process. It is possible to control, through the Listed Building Consent and enforcement action, the execution of schemes that would or do have an adverse impact on the character of historic interiors.

I would suggest that the main factors which can be controlled through the planning process are the preservation of archaeological evidence (paint) either *in situ* or by record, the technical aspect of paint type, and the aesthetic impact of changes in decoration.

References

1 Department of the Environment, Transport and the Regions, Department of National Heritage, *Planning Policy Guidance Note 15: Planning and the Historic Environment*, HMSO, London, 1994.
2 Mynors, C., *Listed Buildings, Conservation Areas and Monuments,* Sweet and Maxwell, London 1999.

Formulating Procedures for Architectural Paint Research

Tina Sitwell

The National Trust is responsible for the care of over 200 houses in England, Wales and Northern Ireland, which includes the conservation of the collections and the historic interiors and exteriors.

Prior to 1995 decisions regarding redecoration were based upon archival information related to the house concerned, relevant academic research for the period, an architectural study of the history of the room in question and paint scrapes (the mechanical removal of layers of existing paint). This information was considered with regard to the furnishings in the room (the furniture, paintings, curtains, carpets, etc.) and their present condition in order to present a holistic approach to the room and its appearance relative to the remaining rooms in the house.

Some paint analysis was undertaken to clarify certain aspects of the decorative history but a systematic approach involving the use of paint analysis and the documentation of the results had not been developed. The National Trust did not have an appointed staff member to oversee paint analysis, nor did it have an in-house facility for analysing paint cross-sections. In 1995 the Trust appointed a part-time Advisor on the Conservation of Painted Surfaces whose function was to oversee the analysis of paint cross-sections in all areas of painted surfaces excluding paintings.

With regard to historic interiors and exteriors, consideration was given to developing a more systematic approach to paint analysis in order to help clarify the paint history of a room and to develop methods for conserving existing schemes or uncovering earlier schemes where possible.

The decision-making process for redecoration or conservation of existing schemes involves numerous people within and outside the Trust. To understand fully how the decision is reached it is necessary to explain this process. The Trust is divided into various regions and each region has a Historic Buildings Representative (HBR) who is responsible for the presentation of the houses and their contents. For redecoration schemes, it is the HBR who initiates the project, seeks funding and collates existing archival information and academic research. The HBR heads the project and liaises with colleagues in different departments and various advisory committee members.

The Advisor on the Conservation of Painted Surfaces and the Advisor on Interior Decoration (an external appointment currently held by James Finlay) consult with the HBR to prepare a programme of investigation. James provides information about the history of the room based on archival information as well as his investigation and study of the architectural changes to the room. He also undertakes paint scrapes to reveal previous painted schemes. The Advisor on the Conservation of Painted Surfaces, in consultation with James and the HBR, recommends a programme of paint analysis and an appropriate paint analyst. A specification is then prepared in liaison with the paint analyst. The Trust does not have in-house facilities for paint analysis and, therefore, contracts the work with private analysts. Where possible we try to establish a relationship between the analyst and a particular house, period or architect. This approach enables the analyst to benefit from a developing in-depth understanding of the house, period or architect, this continuity of research also proves extremely beneficial to The National Trust.

The accumulated information is presented to the Interior Decoration Review Panel which comprises the Director and Deputy Director of the Historic Buildings Department, the Advisor on Paintings and Sculpture, the Advisor on the Conservation of Painted Surfaces, the Architectural Historian, the Advisor on Interior Decoration and other interested parties who are invited to express their opinions. Many views and opinions are discussed at these meetings but the function of the Panel is to provide advice to the HBR based on their presentation.

Consideration is given to the contents of the room (their history and condition) and the historical presentation context of the house in general and the room in particular. It is a holistic approach, which attempts to ensure that the redecoration sits comfortably with the condition of the contents and that the historical presentation is understandable, particularly in rooms where the overall scheme may incorporate decorative changes of several periods.

The following is an example of work in progress which should help to illustrate our working methods more clearly. The Library at Nostell Priory was designed by Robert Adam in 1766 (Figure 8.1). Thomas Ward is known to have worked at Nostell Priory in the 1820s and it is believed that he may have been responsible for the application of a grained bird's-eye maple scheme to the bookcases. There are references to further redecoration work at the house in 1875–6 which do not specify which rooms were redecorated but at least indicate that work was undertaken at that time. The present scheme dates from 1977 when the ceiling was repaired and redecorated following subsidence damage. The room in its present state contains decorative elements from different periods and the ceiling, although painted in an Adam-like manner, does not reflect the original colours nor possibly the colours contemporary with the introduction of the graining on the bookcases.

Fortunately, the original Adam sketches for the design of the Library survive in the archives at the house as does his drawing for the ceiling design (in the Soane Museum). The former drawing being annotated has some inconsistencies which might indicate subsequent changes by him or another hand. A double portrait of Sir Rowland and Lady Winn by Hugh Douglas Hamilton shows the couple standing in the enlarged Library in 1767. A thick discoloured varnish obscured the painting and it has been cleaned in the hope of providing further evidence of the appearance of the original Adam scheme. If possible, paint analysis will be undertaken on the painting to determine if any glazes may have faded which now alter the tonal appearance of certain aspects of the room in the painting, particularly those areas which are now grained.

The original specification for the current architectural paint analysis was to determine the original Adam scheme and the later scheme which corresponds to the introduction of the bird's-eye maple wood-graining. This analysis showed that there were six schemes; the original scheme following closely the original sketches, but that the wood-graining, which was the third scheme applied to the joinery, may have occurred at a date later than 1820. Questions were raised about the various colour schemes for the ceiling and further analysis is currently being undertaken. The final decision about the redecoration of the room is problematic, as the original Adam scheme was substantially altered by the introduction of the wood-graining of the bookcases. Both schemes have historical importance and the final presentation must be a successful compromise of the two schemes. Paint analysis has played an important role in clarifying the various schemes but the final presentation decision has to consider the results in light of the other factors and, dare I say, a degree of subjectivity.

A clear specification for paint analysis is essential if the analyst is to provide the information required. In the past, specifications have been provided on an informal basis either through correspondence or at site meetings. This has not always been satisfactory as the analyst may be unclear about the exact scope of the work and may not have immediate access to all relevant information. There is also a tendency for lack of clarity with regard to the nature of the information in terms of intention and relevance. Several recent projects have proved more successful as they have been team-based in operation with the paint analyst and Trust staff members meeting regularly to discuss results. It also enables the team to understand more clearly the nature of paint analysis, what it can and cannot do, and look at the results from different perspectives as the interpretation of paint analysis is often clarified by information from other sources.

To improve our methodology, a specification form is being devised which outlines the scope of the work, sample locations and all relevant archival and historical information related to the project (Figure 8.2). In addition, the form will include *guidelines* on the documentation. Paint analysts have developed their own documentation forms and it would be difficult to prepare a standard form which would be acceptable to everyone. Therefore, the specification form is crucial as it should clearly identify the scope of the work and the data required. Not only is this essential for ensuring that results will be relevant to the project but also it assists with the transfer of information to the database.

The database is currently being designed by Richard Allen of Bath University and Lisa Oestreicher, a private paint analyst. Prior to the development of the database, Lisa had collated the existing reports which included not only those specifically related to paint analysis but also letters and reports related to past work. A review of this information enabled them to design a system which would incorporate these results and also provide further fields to store information from other sources within the Trust. As the diagram (Figure 8.3) shows, the system is divided into many fields which inter-relate and copy repetitive information to the individual fields. The main field provides a summary of the most relevant information and the

FORMULATING PROCEDURES FOR ARCHITECTURAL PAINT RESEARCH

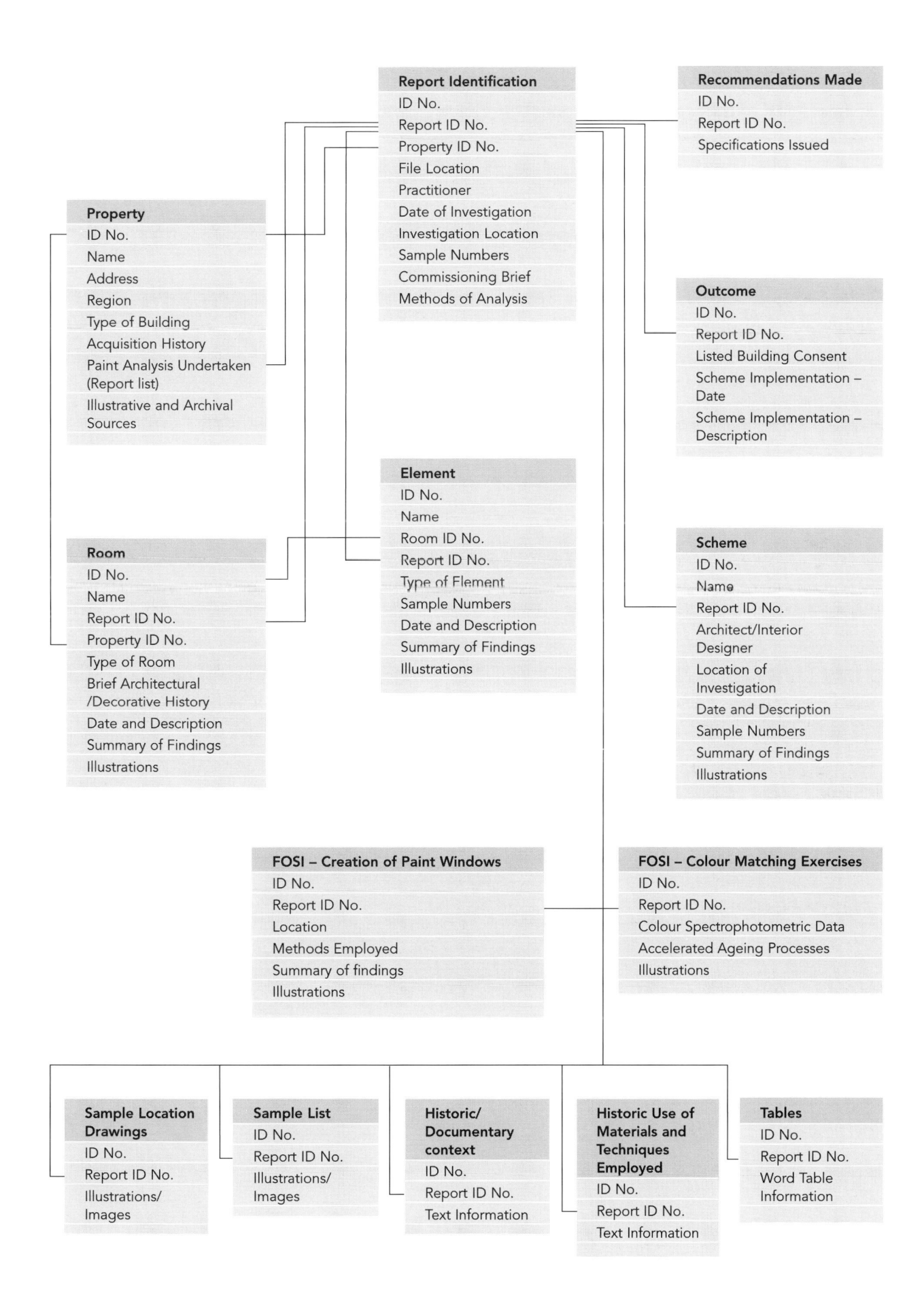

Property
- ID No.
- Name
- Address
- Region
- Type of Building
- Acquisition History
- Paint Analysis Undertaken (Report list)
- Illustrative and Archival Sources

Report Identification
- ID No.
- Report ID No.
- Property ID No.
- File Location
- Practitioner
- Date of Investigation
- Investigation Location
- Sample Numbers
- Commissioning Brief
- Methods of Analysis

Recommendations Made
- ID No.
- Report ID No.
- Specifications Issued

Outcome
- ID No.
- Report ID No.
- Listed Building Consent
- Scheme Implementation – Date
- Scheme Implementation – Description

Room
- ID No.
- Name
- Report ID No.
- Property ID No.
- Type of Room
- Brief Architectural /Decorative History
- Date and Description
- Summary of Findings
- Illustrations

Element
- ID No.
- Name
- Room ID No.
- Report ID No.
- Type of Element
- Sample Numbers
- Date and Description
- Summary of Findings
- Illustrations

Scheme
- ID No.
- Name
- Report ID No.
- Architect/Interior Designer
- Location of Investigation
- Date and Description
- Sample Numbers
- Summary of Findings
- Illustrations

FOSI – Creation of Paint Windows
- ID No.
- Report ID No.
- Location
- Methods Employed
- Summary of findings
- Illustrations

FOSI – Colour Matching Exercises
- ID No.
- Report ID No.
- Colour Spectrophotometric Data
- Accelerated Ageing Processes
- Illustrations

Sample Location Drawings
- ID No.
- Report ID No.
- Illustrations/Images

Sample List
- ID No.
- Report ID No.
- Illustrations/Images

Historic/Documentary context
- ID No.
- Report ID No.
- Text Information

Historic Use of Materials and Techniques Employed
- ID No.
- Report ID No.
- Text Information

Tables
- ID No.
- Report ID No.
- Word Table Information

Figure 8.2 Overview of The National Trust Database for Architectural Paint Research

43

subsequent fields subdivide the information into rooms, elements, schemes and technical data.

The purpose of the database is to create a central registry for all reports as opposed to the present system whereby the information is stored regionally. The system should allow an operator to search for specific information and also make comparative studies of that information. For example, the type and occurrence of graining in various houses, the use of a particular pigment, the decorative treatment of an architectural element in a particular period or the use of an unusual medium. It is hoped that the database will be available to outside organizations and *bona fide* individuals involved in paint research. The project has highlighted several problematic areas such as the necessity for consistency of documentation for ease of transfer of information to the database and to ensure that each project, where possible, provides information for the various fields; the necessity for an accepted thesaurus of architectural terms, materials and pigments and the storage and retrieval of information, particularly visual images.

The National Trust is a large, regionally based organization with limited resources for paint analysis and research into decorative schemes. Its decision making process is broad based and often lengthy in its deliberations. However cumbersome the process, it does undertake redecoration projects seriously and with caution. The use of paint analysis, the development of a specification for its use and the development of a database for storage of information are seen as tools to aid in the decision-making process.

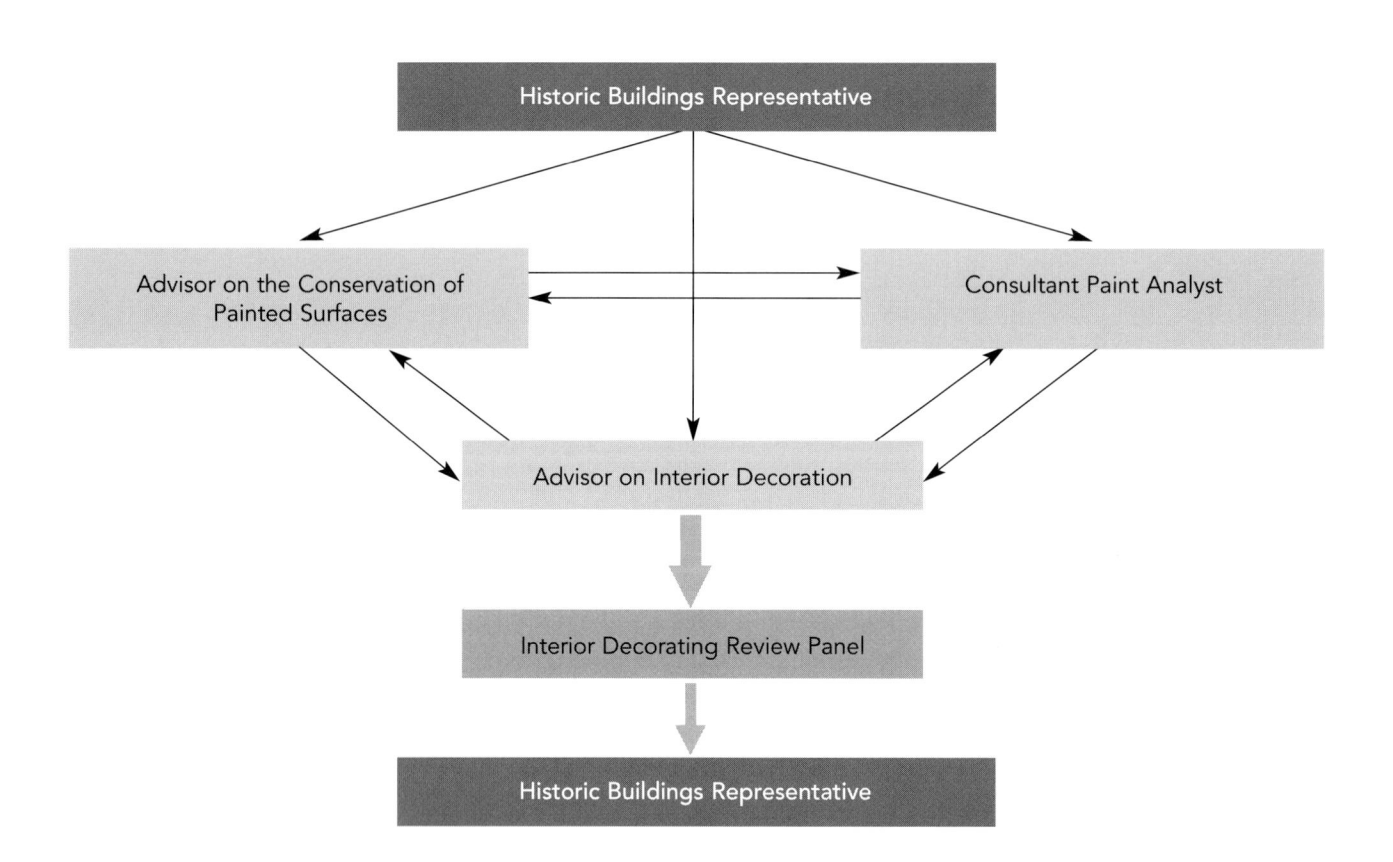

Figure 8.3 National Trust Structure for Paint Analysis

Session 4

Proposed Guidelines for Commissioning Architectural Paint Research

Helen Hughes

Copies of outline drafts of proposed guidelines for commissioning architectural paint research had been circulated to all delegates in advance of the *Layers of Understanding* seminar. This session offered an opportunity for delegates to review the structure and content of the paper.

Each main section of the guidelines was presented and read through. Discussion on various sections of the proposed guidelines was lively and animated. All of the points raised by the delegates will be considered when the guidelines are redrafted. The discussion was extremely valuable as it gave an insight into the major concerns of professional building conservators.

Introduction to the proposed guidelines

Potential of Architectural Paint Research

For well over three hundred years, paint finishes have been repeatedly applied to architectural elements following ordered and systematic procedures using a developing range of materials. Investigation of these accumulated layers of paint and other decorative finishes provides an insight into a building's decorative history, structural development and social history. The accumulated layers of historic paint on historic buildings and architectural elements are an important archaeological resource and, as such, require careful management and conservation.

Over the past 25 years the study of historic paints in England has developed a methodology, and organized projects carried out by the few experienced architectural paint specialists working in this country have increased our understanding of how buildings once appeared, how they were used and how they were altered. It should be remembered that buildings are constructed and altered by people, and an awareness of their motivations, tastes, aspirations and changing fortunes can be critical in achieving an understanding of a building's development. A successful architectural paint investigation may result in a report which gives a narrative account of the building's history, intermeshing the historic documentation and the archaeological evidence with the lives of successive owners.

Problems

Despite these advances the potential of architectural paint research in building documentation and archaeology is still misunderstood and the subject needs to be more clearly defined. There is still an entrenched belief that paint research involves merely the scraping back of paint layers to reveal earlier colours or the identification in analytical laboratories of the pigmentation of isolated paint flakes.

Solutions

Informed and enlightened clients: Conservation professionals who commission architectural paint research have an obligation to be aware of this methodology and current developments as part of their own professional expertise. They should also be aware of changing tastes in the decoration of historic interiors and the impact of cost constraints on the choice of painting materials in previous centuries. More importantly they must have an open-minded approach to the research findings. Most of the historic interiors we see today are decorated to suit modern tastes, not as they once were but how we wish they had been. The architectural paint specialist should have an objective approach to the research and provide accurate and reliable information about the historic schemes. The success of a research project should not be judged by whether the client likes or dislikes a rediscovered historic scheme:[1]

It is impossible to approach the understanding of historic interiors through modern concepts of colour and taste in their redecoration.

It may be a requirement for Listed Building Consent or obtaining grant aid that architectural paint research is carried. In such cases the purpose and scope of the required research must be clearly defined by the regulatory body imposing the requirement.

Training for architectural paint specialists: At present there is no formal training in the field of architectural paint research and no clear consensus as to what service an architectural paint research specialist should provide.

Standards and guidance notes: The discipline of architectural paint research now requires an agreed methodology to ensure that research programmes are carried out in an efficient and systematic manner, and that the subject can develop as a routine procedure of architectural conservation.

Aim of the guidelines

These guidelines are being prepared by the Architectural Paint Research Unit of English Heritage, in collaboration with a wide range of professionals working within the discipline. They are a first attempt to suggest an agreed methodology for the subject and reflect current procedures undertaken by English Heritage and consultants employed by English Heritage when researching historic buildings within our care.

The guidelines aim to provide those involved in the conservation and development of historic buildings with a step-by-step introduction to architectural paint research investigation and the conservation or recreation of historic decorative schemes. They will offer a guide to the working methods and the scope of the service that should be provided by a competent paint research specialist.

The guidelines are not intended to replace the advice given by architectural paint specialists but should be used as a complementary aid. The success of the project is dependant on intelligent sampling and the interpretation of paint stratigraphy. It is hoped that the guidelines will enable those commissioning the research to be more critical of research methods and able to determine whether or not a researcher is following good practice. Experienced architectural paint specialists will be familiar with the procedures outlined but newcomers to the field may find the contents useful in learning the necessary skills.

Definition of architectural paint research

An architectural paint research investigation aims to establish the structural and decorative development of an architectural element, interior, building or structure. It is based on the study of existing records (historical and archaeological) coupled with an examination of the building and paint samples (and other decorative finishes) removed from it. The research will use appropriate methods and practices and will result in a suitable documentation record.

Good architectural paint research will be carried out:

- to inform the conservation, alteration, demolition, repair or management of an architectural element, interior, building or structure
- to establish a better understanding of an architectural element, interior, building or structure
- to produce a record of research findings

Determining the need for architectural paint research

As part of a broader conservation plan or building report

An architectural paint research investigation may offer an understanding of the phases of the building's history and in major projects may be carried out in collaboration with other building specialists such as architectural historians, building analysts or dendrochronologists.

To inform the recreation of an historic scheme

The accurate reconstruction of a period interior will most often be sought in historic house museums or significant listed buildings especially those open to the public. In addition it is often discovered that the understanding of the original scheme and the colours intended by their designers gives unexpected insights into the use of the building and the articulation of its architecture.

To establish the significance of an existing scheme before building repair or redecoration

Important decorative schemes may easily be lost by being overpainted. It is important to bear in mind that decorative schemes, especially in grand interiors, may have been retained for centuries. Should the stripping of historic paint which results in the total destruction of the archaeological record require Listed Building Consent?

Is architectural paint research required?

If the answer to any one of these questions is 'Yes' then appropriate architectural paint research should be commissioned.

Yes	Is there a requirement or a desire to understand aspects of the development of a building?	No
Yes	Is there a need to establish the decorative history of a room or architectural element either for academic interest or with the long-term aim of recreating the historic scheme of a particular period?	No
Yes	Is there a need to establish the significance of an existing decorative scheme before it is stripped off or obliterated by new decorative finishes?	No
Yes	Is there a proposal to remove/strip historic paint?	No
Architectural Paint Research Required		Architectural Paint Research Not Required

The overpainting of existing decorative finishes

If existing paintwork is to be overpainted, an assessment of the significance of this finish should be made. In some properties, lengthy periods of disuse have resulted in the retention of very old layers of paint. In a small number of particularly important interiors decorative finishes have been retained for several hundred years.

The stripping of accumulated paint finishes

Surfaces should always be adequately prepared before redecoration so that they are sound and bondable. Paint losses should be restricted to removal of flaking paint. The removal or stripping of paint layers is an irreversible act which destroys archaeological evidence. Should the stripping of historic paint require Listed Building Consent?

Planning an architectural paint research programme

Stage 1: Formulate research objectives

The aim and needs of the building conservation and/or redecoration should be identified at the outset of the project. It goes without saying that any research required to formulate aspects of the works programme should be completed before works begin. This may mean that the research requires separate funding. It is not sufficient to ask for 'some paint research'.

Stage 1	Formulate research objectives
Stage 2	Assembling existing documentation
Stage 3	Sampling, examination and presentation of interim findings
Stage 4	Formulation of a conservation/redecoration policy
Stage 5	Conservation/redecoration programme
Stage 6	Report and archiving

Stage 2: Assemble existing documentation

The architectural paint specialist should be aware of all existing records related to the building e.g. historic plans, accounts, drawings, photographs and contemporary accounts. These records will inform an effective sampling strategy.

Stage 3: Sampling, examination and presentation of interim findings

A sampling strategy which is based on an assessment of the existing documentation and on-site observation should be agreed before sampling is undertaken. The specialist should remove samples. Presentation of interim findings may be made in report form and/or discussion on site or in the specialist's workplace.

Stage 4: Formulation of a conservation/redecoration policy

The formulation of a conservation and/or redecoration policy is dependent on many factors such as the significance of the research findings, the project aims, time schedules and budgets. In all cases priority must be given to the preservation of existing archaeological evidence. In a small number of projects the exposure of an historic finish may be appropriate. In most cases the specialist will be able to advize on the wide range of options available for the recreation of historic schemes.

Stage 5: Conservation/redecoration programme
The specialist may provide advice on the authentic formulation of historic paints or the use of suitable modern paint finishes and advize on appropriate colour matches.

Stage 6: Report and archiving
A record of the architectural paint research programme should include a summary of the aims and objectives of the research, a record of the analysis of the paint samples and the outcome of the research. Attached appendices should give details of sample location, cross-section reference lists, relevant documentation and details of any significant material analysis carried out.

A copy of the report, appendices and the mounted samples and artefacts removed during the research should be lodged in an approved archive. The sample locations and the mounted samples form an important addition to the primary documentation of a building and may be used to re-evaluate the research findings at a future date.

Architectural paint research procedures

The success of an architectural paint research investigation depends on the ability and experience of the specialist consultant. In a developing field competitive tendering is rarely the best method of selection. Clients should ensure that the appointed specialist is able to demonstrate training and experience which is appropriate to the project. Consultants should not be asked to price per sample, but costs may be broken down in terms of hours spent on site sampling, hours spent in sample preparation, conducting documentary research and expenses incurred.

Preliminary briefing of an architectural paint research specialist
Consultants invited to undertake the project will normally require access to the site to be briefed in greater detail and to assess the project. The researcher should be asked to agree a research plan with the client which will illustrate the understanding of both parties of the existing documentation, the logic of the sampling strategy and the phases of the proposed research.

Basic competencies which should be demonstrated by an architectural specialist
An architectural paint specialist will have a wide range of skills usually have professional training as an architect, conservator, building analyst, archaeologist, material analyst, decorative paint specialist or interior designer. In addition to skills related to their professional training and experience a good architectural paint specialist should be able to demonstrate competency in the following:

- Knowledge of house-painting materials and techniques (historic and modern)
- Architectural history and history of interior decoration
- Basic microscopy
- Analytical techniques for the identification of painting materials
- Conservation codes and practices and building legislation

Procedures forming a normal architectural paint research project
The following core procedures should form part of the majority of architectural paint research projects.

- Assessment of existing documentation
- Examination on site
- Formulation of sampling strategy based on documentation and on site observations
- Removal of paint samples
- Examination of paint samples at low magnification and mounting of samples
- Examination of paint samples in cross-section under high magnification (normal illumination and ultra-violet fluorescence where appropriate)
- Stratigraphic interpretation (with reference to building development)
- Material analysis – the specialist may be able to conduct a fairly wide range of material analysis in-house (microchemical spot tests/media staining/polarizing microscopy)
- In some projects more sophisticated methods of analysis Gas Chromatography and Mass Spectroscopy (GC-MS) and High Performance Liquid Chromatography (HPLC) may be appropriate. The research benefits and cost implications must be discussed with the client. It is essential that all analytical procedures carried out by third parties are clearly identified as such.
- Reports documenting findings and conservation/redecoration options and specifications should be written in a clear, concise and logical style. Technical terms should be explained so that the report is easily understood by the client.

References

1 Bristow, I. C., *Architectural Colour in British Interiors 1615–1840*, Yale University Press, New Haven and London, 1996, p. x.

Discussion Sessions

Chaired by Ian Bristow, Kate Clark and Helen Hughes

The papers presented at the *Layers of Understanding* seminar stimulated animated discussion which covered a wide range of topics from programming and training to the consideration of the usefulness of black and white photographs in determining coloured decorative schemes.

The discussion sessions were recorded and transcribed; these have been collated under appropriate headings. The contributions have been slightly edited but hopefully retain the style of the speakers. Permission for the use of all extracts published has been obtained from all the named contributors.

Proposed guidelines for commissioning architectural paint research

Roger Mears (Conservation Architect)
The phrase 'paint samples (and other decorative finishes) removed from it' which is used in the guidelines may be seen as encouraging the large wholesale removal of rather more than small paint samples. I suggest that this section be reworded to suggest a rather more discreet process.

David McLoughlin
(Principal Conservation Officer, Bath City Council)
I agree with the earlier comment. The term 'removed from' sounds very strong. It may well be that samples are removed from it but perhaps the wording 'coupled with an examination of the building and its paint samples', might be better. Maybe some future technique will evolve which does not involve the physical removal of paint samples.

Stephen Levrant
(Conservation Architect, Heritage Architecture)
There are several things in the guidelines which rather worry me. One is the idea that architectural paint research is carried out as part of a broader conservation plan. I think that this item could lead to some confusion. As you know it is difficult enough to get a client to agree to the preparation of a conservation plan. I feel that a conservation plan might well highlight the need for paint investigation or a research programme, which I think would probably be a separate part of the conservation file on a particular building. I suggest that the paint research is not lumped in with conservation plans for the purposes of the guidelines document as this may lead to even more confusion.

One other point I would like to make. I think the checklist should pose the question 'Have you got the money?' If no money is available to fund the research then it is quite simply not going to be carried out.

Nicholas Thompson
(Conservation Architect, Donald Insall Associates Ltd)
I think the checklist needs to be broken down so that these questions can be applied both to the building as a whole and to elements within the building. In my experience paint research is never an all or nothing situation. Certain parts of the building or certain finishes may be more sensitive than others, while other parts are less problematic. Perhaps the commissioning client should prepare an overview of the significance of finishes in the building first and then decide whether to home in on certain areas in more detail. This chart might be more useful if it provided step-by-step directions to help make an assessment of whether paint research is required. I am sure the guidelines would be useful if they explained the

purpose of paint research and the range of options available for the redecoration of historic interiors. I think what frightens most people is finding themselves in an all or nothing situation. They fear that if they do establish an original decorative scheme, someone is going to force them to go back to the appearance of an interior say 200 years ago, which is totally inappropriate for the present use of the building. I think the guidelines need to be presented as a more understanding and subtly written questionnaire.

Helen Hughes
Identifying areas of supposed significance, which could be proved or disproved by paint analysis, could form the core of a research brief formulated by the client.

Delegate (not identified)
I think it is important to stress that it is not just the original decoration that we are interested in. The purpose of the research is to get an assessment of all the decorative schemes.

Helen Hughes
It is important to establish the significance of all existing schemes. The paint research in the Saloon at Audley End established that the existing scheme dated from the 1770s. All too often people make assumptions about decorative finishes and do not question whether the existing paint decoration is of any importance.

Helen Hughes
We should consider the whole process of taking paint samples and their examination. We are trying to produce a flexible document which can offer guidance for small and large projects. There has to be some form of monitoring of the research and some sort of constant feedback system so that clients are aware of how the research is proceeding. This will also provide opportunities for other buildings analysts who may be working on the same project to benefit from interim findings. It is more than pointless to await the eventual publication of separate specialist reports when immediate access to their preliminary findings may have helped other analysts working on the project. It is in the clients best interest to encourage or devise a system of information pooling.

Delegate (not identified)
It is important to encourage the concept of dynamic research. This was mentioned under monitoring but the historian, paint historian or investigator needs to be able to have the flexibility to come backwards and forwards. They pick up the results of documentary research, look at some of the physical evidence which will then lead to more documentary reset and so on. It is a circle or a process that goes on and on throughout the job and I think it is most important when commissioning this kind of research to recognize that there is a need for constant consultation throughout.

Helen Hughes
Considering Stage 4 (Formulation of a conservation/redecoration policy), ideally we will be using the results of the research to formulate the conservation or redecoration policy. After this stage we can proceed to carry out the actual redecoration programme itself which is Stage 5 (Conservation/redecoration programme). The client may not be able to see the works programme evolving from the findings of the research programme. How many projects seem to start at Stage 5 without any consideration of stages 1, 2 and 3? Perhaps presenting the process in these simple stages will actually bring it home to commissioning clients that there is a logical progression. All too often research and investigation are commissioned when strategic decisions or assumptions have already been made. In many cases the investigation is being carried out while the conservation and redecoration programme is being implemented, by this time we are definitely in Stage 5 of the project.

The final stage, Stage 6 (Report and archiving), is very important. This is an opportunity to draw together all the findings and compile a lasting record of the research and how it was used. The report should contain appendices, diagrams, a mounted sample list. The guidelines have attempted to give some advice on the archiving of reports and samples.

Treve Rosoman (English Heritage)
There has been a lot of discussion about what happens before or during the research project, but very little about what happens afterwards. Stage 6 (Report and archiving) doesn't even mention it. At the end of the project the curator has to look after the building. Our Dutch speaker, Angelique Friedrichs, showed us examples of sample paintboards which were a record of the new paint finishes applied to the rooms. These are incredibly useful to have and really should be produced at the end of each project. Archiving is a big problem: it should be carried out as soon as the work is completed.

Helen Hughes
We work through the project and then abandon it at the end with masses of files and move onto the next project when we really should be making a point of archiving the project.

Treve Rosoman
I think that archiving is also the responsibility of the curator and the facilities manager.

Helen Hughes
Archiving of the mounted paint samples is an issue which should be considered by the client from the

outset of the project. There have been lengthy conversations about this. In many cases paint research specialists would like to keep the mounted samples for comparative references. The samples can be considered as part of their working archive. But on the other hand, the samples actually form part of the documentation of the building. We are trying to reconcile these two factors by suggesting that the mounted samples are the property of the client or the guardian of the building, so they will in effect own the paint samples. However, the paint analyst should have the option of retaining the samples if they can demonstrate that they are going to be kept in an organized archive. Other researchers must be given reasonable access to that archive if they want to look at samples. If the archive is broken up for any reason, the samples will be returned to the building or transferred to another approved archive. Does that sound an acceptable solution? How does The National Trust and its consultants react to that proposal?

Tina Sitwell
The National Trust has discussed whether or not we should keep samples within our conservation section. One problem is that we do not have room to keep samples nor do we have anyone to organize a proper archive. We agreed that we would like access to the samples because there are times when we go back to a scheme and we might actually want to look at the samples taken in 1970. Then we must rely on the paint analysts having archived them properly and stored them properly so they are still useable. At the moment, all the paint analysts who work for the Trust retain their own samples. Perhaps we will have to devise a system whereby we can ensure that they are properly stored and we have easy access to them.

Jane Davies (Jane Davies Conservation)
I recently had a client who was very interested in putting together an archive of the finished work, together with mounted samples, which was very encouraging. A suggestion was made that all of this information together with other larger bits of documentation about the building should be placed in a time capsule and cemented into the floor. This obviously was not an easy access option. Eventually I was able to persuade the client that the samples should be lodged in the English Heritage Architectural Paint Research Archive. This was appropriate as the project had been funded by the Heritage Lottery Fund and monitored by English Heritage.

Helen Hughes
We really need to agree a basic format for reports. Project briefs for architectural paint research carried out on behalf of English Heritage stipulate the format of the final reports. This is a way of imposing a standard on the consultant. If they know that there is a requirement to provide an introduction, a history, a general project background, and that the appendices must contain specific information, that pages and paragraphs must be numbered, then there is a structure within which to work. I think a lot of consultants actually find this report format specification quite helpful.

This guidance is also helpful to new people coming into the field. If we have a workable standard format it would make an assessment of different types of research carried out by different consultants easier for clients to access.

Patrick Baty
What is really needed is not so much a format for the report, but a list of the things to be included. I think it's really more a question of asking what should be in a good report, rather than necessarily the format in which it's going to be presented, which might vary very much from job to job. For instance, if you were working on a major project involving a team of building historians there is very little point in reproducing the building's history in any sort of length. What often happens is that if you are a one-man-show on a building you may have to do the historical research yourself.

Helen Hughes
Even then, if you were working in collaboration with a historian you should include a little summary of their findings, which then puts your paint research into context. All too often I am sent reports which start without dating the building, or giving any background information of the building or room. A given format might just act as a sort of aide memoire to researchers to mention the date of the building, where it is, and stress that a record of the location of the paint samples is very important.

Delegate (not identified)
I just wanted to question the formulation of a conservation/redecoration policy. I would have thought that would have been the job of a conservator rather than a paint analyst.

Helen Hughes
The formulation of the conservation/redecoration policy is really the responsibility of the commissioning client or the project manager who collates the relevant information. The whole purpose of conducting the research is to give them the information so they can use that information to make their own conservation and redecoration policies. So what you are saying is quite right, the architectural paint researcher is not going to formulate the policy – the client should do that. However, it may be that the research findings influence the policy and the paint researcher may have a significant role advizing on the implementation of the conservation or redecoration programme.

David McLoughlin
If that's the case, then Stage 5 (Conservation/redecoration programme) needs to provide advice on who to go to for this sort of expertise. It might be helpful to define what can be done by a conservator, what needs to be done by an architectural paint researcher, what by a historian. When this guidance document is finally published I think it would be very helpful to have actual illustrations, for example the strata diagrams produced by Pamela Lewis which compared the stratification of different paint samples one to another were very informative, and would be very helpful to show readers.

Helen Hughes
The final document will be an approximately 16 page booklet with colour photographs and cross-sections. It will include examples of previous research and brief case studies and hopefully it will be user friendly.

Delegate (not identified)
I think I should draw attention to two already existing English Heritage publications which are models of their kind. One is the *Conservation Areas Appraisal*, which clearly defines the special architectural or historic interest of Conservation areas and the other one is the Government Historic Buildings Advisory Unit's advisory leaflet *The Care of Historic Buildings and Ancient Monuments*.[1,2] This contains the brief outlining what is required for inspections. I think that if one is looking for a way of setting out guidelines which does exactly say to a researcher or analyst, you will write a, b, c, this is an absolutely wonderfully model to follow.

Ian Bristow
The important thing we have to bear in mind is the wide spectrum of projects that the guidelines will have to encompass.

Reclamation of obliterated finishes

Delegate (not identified)
I think we should differentiate between paint stripping as preparation to redecoration, and paint stripping to reveal an earlier decorative scheme. I think these are two very different issues. When is paint removal valid and acceptable?

Helen Hughes
I agree that these issues should be addressed separately.

Stripping away of all existing painted decorations to reveal the details and sharp profiles of mouldings of a substrate, often without any analysis of the layers being removed, is one process. The careful removal of specific paint layers by a conservator to reveal or reclaim an earlier painted decoration is another entirely different process. In both cases there needs to be a careful assessment of the significance of the painted decorations that are being lost. These should be fully recorded before they are removed.

Allyson McDermott
(Wallpaper Conservator, Allyson McDermott Restoration)
We have a particular problem with Tynecastle tapestries, which are embossed wallpapers intended to be overpainted. If you continue to overpaint these wallpapers you lose more and more of the definition of the pattern, but if you strip away the paint layers you will lose the original scheme. So how do you approach this problem? I think this has to be dealt with separately from the other issues.

Wallpapers

Treve Rosoman
I would like to put in a special plea for wallpapers. In many cases the wallpaper has already gone before any paint analysis is undertaken. Once you have lost the wallpaper you have lost the greater part of your decorative scheme.

Helen Hughes
I agree that this is a great problem. Once the wallpaper is removed the important junctions and overlaps of paint and paper which would help relate the joinery decoration to the wallpaper have also been lost.

Treve Rosoman
There is some interesting work being carried out by Margaret Pritchard at Colonial Williamsburg in the USA. She is attempting to relate the colour of woodwork to missing wallpapers. I think that it is very easy for consultants to overlook the importance of wallpapers in the decoration of historic interiors. There is a tendency to simply strip them off and proceed with redecoration.

Helen Hughes
I think the case studies described by Angelique Friedrichs clearly illustrated the benefits of taking a more holistic approach to historic interiors. Problems arise if paint analyst and wallpaper analyst do not work together. The original owner of the house designed all the decorative elements to work together, and so it makes no sense to study the component parts of the scheme in isolation. Last year Allyson McDermott and I ran a joint seminar that attempted to promote this approach to the study of historic interiors. I think the guidelines should stress that other decorative finishes such as wallpapers, gilding, tiling, glass and even door furniture should be considered as forming part of the decorative scheme.

Reversibility

Helen Hughes (in response to a request for a definition of 'obliteration')
By obliteration I mean the simple application of new paint over existing paint finishes so that they are obscured from view. The earlier paint finishes are still there and in theory could actually be reclaimed by removing the overpaint from the surface, but it is never the same as having a pristine and unpainted surface. When we are working in buildings that have not been redecorated for 50 years or so, we might actually be looking at decorative finishes that are of some age. James Edgar mentioned in his talk that to find untouched painted schemes that are earlier than the 1950s or 1960s is becoming increasingly rare. I hope that by stressing this in the guidelines we might highlight this issue and persuade building custodians to determine the significance of all existing paint finishes. We really need house custodians to go through the process of double-checking and giving some consideration to what it is they are obliterating when they redecorate.

We should stress that everyone here today could be called a buildings' conservator, and the bottom line of being a professional conservator is taking responsibility for your actions. If you are recommending or undertaking a process which is not reversible you really must be fully aware of the long-term consequences of your instructions.

Peter Hoffer
(Conservation Architect, Donald Insall Associates Ltd)
Are any decorative schemes reversible? Modern acrylic paints applied on existing painted systems of whatever kind are not readily reversible – or their removal may damage the coats underneath. Is there any reversible paint system?

Ian Bristow
I may be able to offer an answer to this question. I worked some years ago on the drawing room of Lansdowne House, which is now in the Philadelphia Museum of Art. The room was dismantled and taken to the United States in the 1930s and was re-erected in the museum in the early 1940s during the Second World War. Once within the museum it was treated as a 'museum object' which was rather a novel experience. The museum wanted to ensure that, at any time in the future, the room could be returned to the state in which it had arrived in the museum. The decision was therefore taken that the backgrounds of the painted arabesques on the ceiling were to be carefully retouched using water soluble artists' gouache which could be washed off at any time. The joinery throughout the room was painted in acrylic paints which provided a more durable finish. This is removable in acetone, although it would be a much more laborious task than the removal of the gouache. So certainly in that one very special instance, reversibility had been thought about, but my guess is that with the majority of historic rooms it is not feasible to redecorate using reversible materials. With the likelihood that solvent-based materials will be phased out over the next decade, it must be borne in mind that vinyl emulsions are often particularly difficult to remove.

Allyson McDermott
We have carried out several projects where we have used water-based paints to retouch interiors; it has worked very successfully. I would not use gouache because I am somewhat concerned about the long term properties with discolouration that gouache displays. But our major problem is working in an interior that has not got sufficient environmental control. As humidity levels tend to rise, particularly if you are dealing with outside walls for instance, a water-soluble retouching is very unsatisfactory because it does exactly what it is supposed to do; it washes off. This has always been a factor to be taken into account in a decision to use a water-soluble paint. There are difficulties in using reversible paint systems. We have had some success with using very fine Japanese paper as an interleaving barrier between layers of overpaint. This is particularly successful on very pliable wallpaper substrates.

Helen Hughes
I suppose one of the advantages of using traditional paint systems such as lead-based paints in interiors, is that because of their durability and attractive ageing characteristics perhaps the interiors will not have to be redecorated. We saw how long the late eighteenth-century paint in the Saloon at Audley End had survived and it is still serviceable. Perhaps using traditional paint might be a way of avoiding the redecoration cycle and build-up of thick alkyd resin paints which we are currently experiencing.

Richard Ireland (Conservator, Period Restoration)
I just wanted to add a comment about obliteration or rather just simple redecoration. Painting over an existing decorative scheme usually requires a substantial amount of preparation. This can involve an amount of light abrasion or sanding which can be exceedingly destructive especially if the substrate is weak or friable. Were you to remove the most recently applied paint, you might find that you had shaved off most of the early paint, or certainly had damaged many of the upper layers which might well be of significance. So one perhaps should assess whether it would be best to apply a barrier layer to ensure that the existing layers are protected.

Helen Hughes
English Heritage have been working at Bolsover Castle recently where we have established that original early seventeenth-century paint finishes had been unknowingly retained until they were crudely overpainted in 1976. We have spent thousands of pounds removing this modern paint. Had just a little care and consideration been shown in the 1970s this exquisite finish which was in very good condition would have been retained. Although we managed to remove the later paint from the surface of the seventeenth century the original paint it was evident that the original scheme had been sanded down prior to redecoration.

Paint stripping

Stephen Levrant
You have suggested in the draft document (guidelines) that Listed Building Consent should be obtained before any paint is removed from historic buildings. To be honest I am very worried about this proposal as I think it would meet with a great deal of hostility from those involved with carrying out works within historic buildings. Could I ask Helen to clarify this point?

Helen Hughes
To be honest, the suggestion that paint stripping should require Listed Building Consent was included to provoke this very debate. This is a contentious issue as there seems to be a general assumption that it is good practice to remove all traces of old paint before new paint is applied. This assumption has resulted in the loss of large amounts of archaeological evidence and would not be countenanced in any other branch of conservation. We should really highlight this problem. Perhaps we should start with the premise that paint stripping should not be carried out unless it can be justified.

Michael Turner
(Historic Buildings Inspector, English Heritage)
Just to add to the point that Stephen Levrant has just raised. Total or even partial stripping of paint from an element is very destructive because we are destroying evidence of the history of that element and once it has gone that evidence is irreplaceable.

John Nevin (Painter and Decorator, Nevin of Edinburgh)
In fact there are very few specifications which call for the complete removal of paint. When a painter does remove paint it is because it totally failed and is flaking off and cannot be retained. There is usually no need to strip paint that is in good condition. But there does come a point when the accumulated paint reaches a certain thickness and the paint has to come off.

Helen Hughes
So you are thus suggesting that you are happy to paint over existing paint layers as long as they provide a firm bondable surface for further paint layers?

John Nevin
There will certainly be areas of sound paint in any room, in fact I do not think there is a room we have ever worked in where we actually had to strip the whole thing. There does come a time when you physically remove the paint because if you paint over the top you are just adding more layers and extra weight and the flaking will become much worse. In these cases you may want to strip the room to a certain degree, I am not saying strip it entirely. The only reason I have ever seen for stripping a whole room is to recover the architectural detail. So what do you sacrifice, the paint layers or the architectural detail?

Janet Brough (Conservator, Brighton Pavilion)
I think the suggestion that paint stripping should require Listed Building Consent is a good idea.

Cathy Proudlove
The problem of paint stripping is a big issue and requires further discussion. I am actually researching this issue at the moment and have left copies of a discussion paper with the speaker. Please contact me if you are interested in this issue (See Appendix II).

Substrates

David McLoughlin
Every time our local Diocesan Advisory Committee discusses paint finishes in the context of historic churches, the major issue is paint permeability. I do not know how paint permeability is assessed – I am here because I would like to learn. I think it would be very helpful to discuss this issue and to refer to it in the guidance document.

Simon Swann (Plaster Conservator)
During today's discussion there has been no consideration of the substrates onto which the paint is applied. I am a plaster conservator and therefore concerned with plaster, but we should be considering paint applied to wood and metal. Obviously we need to consider what paint is appropriate for each type of substrate. I think there is a danger that that we are removing the discussion of paint out of the context of the rest of the building.

Jane Davies (Jane Davies Conservation)
As a historic paint researcher with a general building conservation background I think any good architectural paint researcher would comment, as a matter of course, on the substrate. You cannot put oil paint on

a fresh lime-plaster surface, for example, and you certainly would not suggest putting a different type of paint such as oil onto a surface that has never been painted with that material before. So I agree that these substrate issues do need to be considered, as they are important, but properly qualified researchers will keep these considerations in mind.

Funding and programming

Fiona Alladyce (Conservator, Historic Scotland)
I agree with many of Helen's views but I think there was one item she mentioned in passing, but did not elaborate on, which was the problem of funding. Certainly in Historic Scotland we find that the whole research investigation is requested on the back of funding which is specifically given with the specification that the client must recreate the original paint scheme. This seems to me a back to front approach and means that the whole focus of the funding is possibly misdirected. It does seem that the whole impetus for requesting paint investigation is simply that without this information a grant will not be offered.

The ideal, surely, would be that paint investigation is funded independently and is carried out for its own sake to provide a fuller understanding of the building rather than for the end product, which is a recreation of an historic paint scheme.

Clients as you know often ignore research findings if the historic schemes are not to their taste. As Helen Hughes mentioned earlier the recreated scheme is often of little significance, clients may well 'paint it whatever colour they like'. The important aspect of the research should be to establish the historic schemes.

Kate Clark
So you see the problem originating with the terms of the grant. Do other people have similar experiences or is that an unmitigated example of what's happening?

Janet Brough
Certainly it has been my experience that the research projects I have been asked to conduct were just hoops that the clients jumped through to get the grants. It is often that case that what you are asked to do is ludicrous when viewed alongside other things that are happening to the object. For instance, being asked to devote a lot of time to analysing paint on historic lamp standards in a park. These lamps were originally lit by gas but they will in the future be lit by electricity. The whole restoration programme for the lamp standards was not well thought through. Finally when the paint research was completed it was planned to strip the lamp standards.

Kate Clark
So you are saying that the underlying problem is actually the conservation philosophy.

Janet Brough
Not enough time is given to the research and the pressure is on to get the money and get the job done. If the clients are seen to jump through the hoop, they have achieved their objective.

John Nevin
We were recently approached by a local authority to put together a paint scheme for a major interior. At the time the hall had already been two thirds painted. We gave them a price for making 60 cross-sections. The architects actually came back to us asking if we could cut the number of samples down to five! Perhaps I must stress that this was one of the principal public buildings in Scotland. They wanted a reduction to five samples to cut costs but ensure that they had some kind of report to show their bosses. That's as bad as it gets.

Kate Clark
So there is no understanding of the purpose of the research work.

John Nevin
Absolutely none!

David Gibson
(Conservation Architect, David Gibson Architects)
I am a devotee of paint cross-sections. The problem I have is different from the one discussed at this seminar. I work in Islington where we have just two Grade I listed buildings and 4,000 Grade II listed buildings. The majority of my work is in fairly simple buildings, but historically fascinating. However, when working for instance on a shop in Caledonian Road, we simply can't afford to do the kind of analysis discussed at this seminar. So I am afraid I have taken to carrying out this analysis by taking five or six samples from the building, embedding them in resin and grinding them off in my kitchen. It does seem to me that while we do need very detailed analysis we also need a system with a quick and rapid response. I find it quite useful and informative because I already have an understanding of what the buildings are about. With a fairly quick, simple analysis I can make decisions and make informed comments about the kinds of colours I find. I think as well as these complex detailed analysis, we do need a quick rapid response system so we can find out very quickly what simple buildings are like, without having to spend very large sums of money doing some research, because we simply haven't got the money.

Kate Clark
This is a particularly important point because we are having a discussion about standards. This is a call for a quick solution to paint research in under-funded properties, but this needs to be mindful of Ian Bristow's concern that quality is essential. It is very important for the co-ordination and management of projects to take this into account.

Use of black and white photographs

Ronan Jeffrey (Shoreditch Town Hall Trust)
I would like to emphasize the importance of historic black and white and sepia photographs. Is anyone doing any work on correlating the rendition of coloured decorations in early black and white photographs?

Helen Hughes
This is an interesting subject. Some research has been carried out in the USA that suggests that the use of black and white photographs to determine the tonality of historic colours can be problematic.[3] The appearance of the final photograph can be affected by various factors such as type of film, developing techniques and lighting and surface reflection. It was established that light yellows could actually appear as dark grey while darker colours might appear to be lighter.

Scrapes versus samples and mounted cross-sections

Peter Hoffer
I have two questions. What are the comparative costs of paint scrapes against the cost of taking samples and examining them in cross-section? Is one much more expensive than the other?

If there is no documentation how do you establish from a cross-section where there are stencil patterns such as the one found in the Dining Room at Kenwood?

Helen Hughes
It takes a great deal of time and effort to carry out a meticulous paint scrape and to make an on-site assessment without the aid of good light and high magnification. The basic cost of getting an expert on site, arranging access to the room with appropriate scaffolding and lighting is the same, whether the consultant takes samples or makes paint scrapes. Working at Osborne House recently we spent three days on-site having planned a sampling strategy in advance and removed and recorded the location of over 300 paint samples from all the elements in several major rooms. These samples are now stored in our studio. After a preliminary examination of them under low magnification we may not think it necessary to mount all the samples to establish the decorative history of these interiors. But the mounted and unmounted samples are now a valuable record of the decorative finishes of Osborne House and have increased the documentation of the interiors. They are of value to the present and any future investigation of the building. This sampling exercise need not be repeated and I would say this was an effective use of time and resources.

To answer your second question, how do we establish the presence of underlying stencil schemes or other patterned decoration without the benefit of documentation? If several samples taken from the same wall face display anomalous stratigraphies then this may suggest that some elaborate scheme may have been applied at some date. At Danson House, examination of paint samples removed from a domed ceiling indicated that a more elaborate, almost painterly, finish had been applied at an early date. This instigated further research which revealed that the panel beds of the dome had originally been decorated in an extremely sophisticated *trompe l'oeil* scheme. There was no documentation of this hitherto unknown scheme. An experienced analyst will certainly be able to distinguish an early grained or marbled decoration from the appearance of the cross-section.

Ian Bristow
Stencil decorations often show up very well in raking light. One is often able to find an elaborate stencil scheme that survives beneath later overpaint, simply by examining a wall face in raking light. I have done something similar in the apse at St. Paul's, Deptford, where the outlines of now-removed boards, probably bearing the Ten Commandments, could be seen in raking light.

Roger Tidbury (Lecturer, Portsmouth University)
There seems to be a reluctance to use the word 'scrape'. Obviously paint scrapes are made on occasions where layers of paint are to be removed to expose the pattern of stencilling, graining or marbling. Is there a term preferred to the word 'scrape'?

Patrick Baty
I would have thought the term 'revelation' or 'exposition' would be more appropriate. I would avoid the use of the term 'scrape' to describe this investigatory process.

Tina Sitwell
Our team was set up by The National Trust. We are trying to educate people in the advantages of taking proper paint analysis. Certainly in The National Trust we have a tradition of making paint scrapes and that continues. We are, however, taking more and more paint samples in conjunction with paint scrapes. This

is a learning exercise for us and I think we have to be careful not to alienate our colleagues. I think we have to be very careful about how we do refer to the issue of paint scrapes, looking at the value as well, rather than just trying to criticize them.

Training

Kate Clark
Angelique Friedrichs' paper has provided a very useful European perspective. I was very interested to note that the conservation course on decorative historic interiors at Maastricht lasts in effect for five years.

Tina Sitwell
We have had the pleasure of working with students from Maastricht on two projects; Angelique was with us last summer and a former colleague Ruth Jongsma did some splendid work at Knole. I must say we were increasingly impressed with the quality and level of dedication of the students, particularly working in National Trust properties which is not an easy experience. I just hope that we can collaborate with the Maastricht course in the future, or even begin a similar training course in this country.

Programming and risk management

John Edwards (Project Manager, Cardiff Castle)
A question for Ian Jardin on the control of risk. Obviously the more research we carry out the smaller the eventual risk. Where conservation is concerned, rather than redecoration, there will still remain an element of risk. What mechanisms does English Heritage deploy to control that risk, for example do you start delegating risk down to contractors; do contractors carry out the work?

Ian Jardin
Risk is of course a big question in any building project and the most important thing to control, but I do think it depends on the nature of the risk. Generally I don't think we are perfect, and in some ways we are still learning. The answer to most risk management is to try to identify it and deal with it as early as possible. With research, as I said during my presentation, I think the answer is to get the research carried out as early as possible so that we can respond to it. But what is also important when dealing with risk, is the notion of contingency plans and allowances. John Nevin (Nevin of Edinburgh) made a point earlier that was relevant; if you don't allow us sufficient contingency to do it properly in the first place, then you are in a mess. There is a terrible pressure on project managers, not to allow sufficient contingencies. That's certainly one of the problems.

Kate Clark
You can control risk again by involving the analyst and historian in advance of and during the actual project work.

Ian Jardin
That's a very good point. To be honest I don't think we involved the research team as fully and as early as we should have done at Danson House and that's the lesson we learned. But I think it's also true to say that involvement doesn't end once the initial research is done. I stress the word reiterative; I think research is something that carries on. So having said you do it as early as possible one thing I am sure about building research generally is that it's not a complete open and shut story, you always learn more. One lesson I have always applied is that it is as important to identify what you don't know as what you do know. There is always a point beyond which there is something that you still don't know, and so the involvement of the research team throughout a project is important.

Unidentified delegate
I agree with everything you said, but I think the danger lies with clients who employ project managers who are used to new build projects, they like to control that risk these days by delegating things down to contractors. They are not really willing to look at contingencies and control the input of professionals as the project progresses because they see in that an element of uncertainty about where it will lead. The point is about education; many of us you are preaching to are the converted, to some extent. It's preaching to the people who are not here that becomes a major issue.

Kate Clark
This is certainly a point which came up in many of the papers. The Guidelines need to be addressed not just to practitioners, but to a much wider audience of project managers and funding bodies, because that seems to be where some of the problems are arising.

Ian Jardin
I have pointed out that one risk factor in a project is making a discovery at a late stage which demonstrates that the project should have been handled differently from the start.

Elizabeth Hirst (Hirst Conservation)
On the subject of research teams, I find quite often that a project co-ordinator, whether an architect or another professional, might have involved an historian, but the paint researcher will not necessarily have any contact with him. A lot of information is not made available unless the paint researcher is assertive in seeking it out. On other projects there is often no one other than the paint analyst (to carry out historical study), so the paint researcher is expected to take on

many roles. This is a problem of education: clients do not know what to expect (of a paint researcher). The seminar must find a means to preach to them.

Ian Jardin
Bodies such as English Heritage or The National Trust can deploy researchers in teams of the kind we used at Danson House, but the private or commercial client will not be able to do this. Ideally there should be a team made up of independent people of equal professional standing: the archaeologist, the architect, the paint researcher. On smaller projects of course that's not practicable, and the usual primary need, understandably, and I think rightly, is probably for the architect. Certainly when we form project teams at English Heritage we should employ paint researchers directly. They should not come to us, as too often they come to private clients, via the architect.

Patrick Baty
What I find is that it often takes a great deal of time and effort to persuade clients to pass over relevant documentation.

Kate Clark
So the problem is not with work not being done but that communication lines are not established.

Delegate (not identified)
This is a problem because we work with historians who don't understand why paint researchers would need to have access to this information: Patrick Baty mentioned this in his talk. They just don't make the connection that paint researcher can actually interpret bills or the history of the family, and that this information will actually have some relevance to the investigation of the paint. People sometimes get the impression that paint researchers are interested only in the physical aspects of paint and don't realize how important it is to integrate all of the existing documentation.

Patrick Baty
Communication, and the fact that one is working often in isolation are the problems. I believe very strongly, as several people have pointed out, that paint researchers should be working as part of a team, we should pass information backwards and forwards because everyone is part of that team. If you work in isolation it feels extremely vulnerable and you also feel as though you haven't got the facts and, as I said in my talk, the work becomes almost an initiative exercise. You sometimes feel as though the client does have relevant information but they are testing you, which isn't very helpful at all.

Conservation policies

Stephen Levrant
Is this discussion 'fiddling while Rome burns'? Government policy is currently directing the way a lot of people like myself work. We now have new ideas about embracing the concept of prime contracting, in which the putting together of teams dealing with very, very important buildings is not only based on the lowest tender, but is the responsibility of project managers who desperately need educating in the concept of teams of specialists, an idea at present met with looks of horror and disbelief. The problem is much deeper than our arguments for specialist teams: there is policy which is pushing us further and further away from this concept. We are at the cutting edge of trying to find a practicable solution: it's a very, very difficult situation and unless it is worked out properly we will never get a consensus.

Kate Clark
Can I respond to that? I am in a small way involved in the current heritage review that English Heritage is undertaking.[4] One of the issues for that review is looking at how heritage management is affected by wider policies. Now it certainly might be in terms of whether these are transport or environment policies, but obviously policy in the building construction world is also hampering how we do our work.

Samples sent through the post

David Hodges (Nimbus Conservation)
On a practical level I think we are all aware of the ideal of involving researchers at an early stage. In real life that's often not possible. In terms of funding and time, its often not feasible to invite a paint analyst to visit a small impoverished church in the middle of Wales to examine peeling paint in the chancel. What do analysts think about being sent samples through the post? – with a brief description of what the samples are and their provenance – even though the analysts have not been able to see the buildings concerned or to make an examination themselves, and not enough samples may have been taken?

Ian Bristow
My first comment is that the quality of sample is just as vital to the success of the research as expertise in looking at it under the microscope. Sample preparation too is terribly important, and of course that starts with the sample taking. I think one can get much more from paint samples if one has seen the rooms concerned. In fact you can get so much more of the feel for the room if you have been there. An isolated sample, taken by someone else may pose problems; has it come from an area of the room that's been replastered,

has it come from an area which has been stripped? I do think it's very important that one should actually see the room and I am generally rather unhappy about looking at samples sent to me through the post.

Helen Hughes
One sample sent to me through the post was a big lump of plaster. I was asked to analyse the black finish on the surface. I was eventually able to visit the property and I discovered that the sample had been taken from a room which had been damaged in a fire. The black finish was actually black charred paint and soot on the surface of the sample. When I examined the room I found that there were a few historic photographs showing the appearance of the room before the fire. These showed a grained scheme, which had been charred by the fire. On that occasion I think a site visit set everything in context.

Kate Clark
Are you both arguing that it is better to do nothing than to do it badly?

Ian Bristow
For 25 years, since I started to use cross-sections, I have felt that you can be certain when it's impossible to interpret a cross-section. In the case of a scrape, unsupported by a cross-section, you have no idea whether you have got the right answer or the wrong answer. For that reason, I think scrapes are dangerous. I think it's very important to find correct solutions because we owe it to the public to have taken pains to ensure that we have done the best that we can.

References

1. English Heritage *Conservation Areas Appraisal,* March 1997.
2. Government Historic Buildings Advisory Unit's advisory leaflet *The Care of Historic Buildings and Ancient Monuments: Guidelines for Government Departments and Agencies,* English Heritage, 1998.
3. Snyder, J.W., Parkes, B.W. and Staehli, A.M, 'Historic Photos as an Aid to Paint Analysis', an unpublished paper presented at the Annual Conference of the Association of Preservation Technology, held in Boston USA, 5–8 October 1988.
4. English Heritage, *Power of the Place: The Future of the Historic Environment,* English Heritage, London, 2000.

Conclusion

Kate Clark

It is perhaps the mark of a successful conference that at its end we realize how much we have learnt since the start of the day. We have had a wonderful range of presentations. The issues discussed today included the importance of teamwork, quality assessments, monitoring the destruction of the resource, evaluation, assessments, archiving and storage. I could have discussed the very same set of issues had I spent the day with a roomful of building archaeologists, or architectural historians, or documentary historians, or wall paint conservationists, or dendrocronlogists, or indeed the myriad of other specialists whose working lives are spent trying to understand buildings. So may I make a plea that all building analysts begin to work together, so that we can begin to learn from each others' experiences and mistakes. I think archaeologists and architectural paint researchers in particular share a lot of common ground.

Today's discussions have included a wide range of projects from the literally 'quick and easy paint scrape' to the detailed analysis carried out by Ian Bristow. We have had a plea for standards and quality from Helen Hughes, not just for consultants but for commissioning clients too, which I thought was a particularly interesting point. We have heard over and over again of the importance of teamwork, not only between architects and architectural historians, but also between paint researchers, project managers and those who actually work on-site. We also heard a plea for education and training, a very important issue which perhaps needs to be discussed in the future. Angelique Friedrichs' paper perhaps provided a model for this, outlining the unique training course provided in The Netherlands.

We have touched on data management and databases, reports, archives and the importance of publication. Ian Bristow's books are fabulous but we need more information on this subject. If we do not get research findings out into the public realm how are people going to learn?

Bubbling away behind all of this is a demand for greater clarity of thought on conservation legislation which was eloquently provided by James Edgar in his discussion of PPG 15. But some big questions of restoration still remain: why do we do it, when do we do it and under what circumstances? I think everything we have been saying today has been touching on these big issues.

I think there is huge potential in using building research findings for visitor interpretation. Understanding buildings is enormous fun, something that I think we can bring to a much wider audience.

There were two missing voices today; one was the voice of craftsmen. I would have liked them to have shared their knowledge of how buildings are built and changed through time. Another voice that I didn't hear today was that of house-owners. They after all are the people on whom we rely to care for the buildings. They are very important; we need to communicate and work with them.

So that is my impression of what I thought was a very interesting and very special seminar. I would like, on behalf of Ian Bristow and myself, to thank not only the people who presented papers, but all who attended for being so willing to take an active part in the discussion and in reacting to the proposed guidelines. Please write and give us your comments. There is no point in English Heritage producing guidelines if they are not acceptable to the practitioners in the field.

I am going to end with a quotation:[1]

(the) reconciliation of the voices of the past and the future with the obvious necessities of everyday life today demands much more than considerable sums of money which in themselves can be a recipe for disaster. It requires understanding depth as well as breadth, a detailed archaeological, historical and ecological appreciation of why what is there is there, a conscious ability to exercise restraint and a dedication to doing nothing when nothing might be the right answer, but above all, a sense of humility.

This was written in 1977 and the author was a young man called Neil Cossons.[2] With that plea for humility I will leave you.

References

1 Cossons, N., *Ironbridge: Landscape of Industry*, Cassell, London, 1977.
2 Sir Neil Cossons became Chairman of English Heritage in April 2000.

Appendices

Appendix 1

Architectural Paint Research Chart and Categorization System

Helen Hughes

The Architectural Paint Research Chart

The Architectural Paint Research Unit (APRU) of English Heritage has devised a systematic approach to conducting its research and presenting its findings in a chart form. The chart can also be used to present findings and monitor the research findings during the research programme.

The Architectural Paint Research (APR) Chart collates main research findings and presents the successive decorative schemes. It has proved to be very popular with project managers and has been adopted by consultants commissioned by English Heritage.

Architectural paint research projects may vary greatly depending not only on the age and status of the building, room or architectural element but also on the amount of physical and documentary evidence which survives. To rationalize each project the APRU at English Heritage has introduced the use of a grid or chart to help collate and assess the various types of information which are pertinent to specific research projects. The chart is developed throughout the project and can be used to update project managers about the state of the research and share new findings with other building analysts.

An empty grid should be drawn up at the beginning of the research project. The cells of the grid will be filled as the project progresses. The final version of the chart should summarize the social, structural and decorative development of the building/room or architectural element. It is probable that the grid will have to be redrawn and modified as the project progresses.

A hypothetical case study – the Saloon – has been used to illustrate how the chart is developed.

APR Chart – 1st stage
Assessment of all documentary evidence to determine main phases (*i.e. changes in occupancy or significant structural alterations*)

At this stage all the documentary evidence which is available should be collated. Much of this evidence may be provided by the historian, house-owner or curator. However the architectural paint researcher

APR Chart 1st stage

Main Phases	Documentation	Events
Phase 6	Present condition/ photograph	Windows inserted west wall 1965
Phase 5	Photograph 1900	Addition of dado rail post 1900
Phase 4	Press/painters' bills	Repairs after fire of 1860
Phase 3	Invoices/accounts	Major refurbishment of interiors 1832
Phase 2	Auction notice	Sale of house 1800
Phase 1	Building accounts/plans	Fitting out of room 1760

must act as a prompt, listing all types of documentation which the historian may have overlooked or not considered relevant to an investigation of decorative schemes. These include building accounts, inventories, sales catalogues and of course paintings and photographs of the room or building.

At this stage it may be possible to suggest main phases when changes or alterations were carried out. These phases are usually associated with changes of occupancy, alterations of wealth or status, family events, historical events or accidents such as fires or storms. In some cases there is no documentation relating to the building and the investigation of the building will be based on surviving fabric (see APR Chart – 2nd stage).

APR Chart – 2nd stage:
Assessment of architectural elements and main phases to devise a sampling strategy

A careful examination of the room itself will provide information about changes to the building. In our hypothetical case it is evident that the fire of 1860 had a great impact on the appearance of the room, damaging the skirting. Other alterations include the addition of the dado rail post 1900 and the creation of a new window in the west wall in 1965.

The chart can be modified to illustrate the loss of original elements and the addition of new ones. The empty cells of the chart pose the question 'How were each of these elements decorated during the main phases of the building's history?'

APR Chart – 3rd stage:
Analysis of paint samples removed from the room

The third stage of the chart will be added after the paint samples have been removed from the selected areas and examined under high magnification. At this stage some pigment or media analysis may have been carried out to clarify the dating or possibly the original appearance of a selected decorative scheme.

The stratigraphy of paint samples from the Saloon can then be incorporated into the chart.

Using the combined findings of the documentary research, building analysis and examination of the paint samples removed from the room, it should be possible to suggest the decorative history of the room and identify any significant decorative finishes of architectural elements.

APR Chart 2nd stage

Main Phases	Elements to be sampled					
	Ceiling (ceiling rose 1860)	**Cornice**	**Wall face**	**Skirting** (replaced after 1860 fire)	**Dado rail** post 1900	**Window** inserted 1965
Phase 6 1965						
Phase 5 1900						
Phase 4 1860 – post fire						
Phase 3 1832						
Phase 2 1800						
Phase 1 1760						

APR Chart 3rd stage

Main Phases	Elements to be sampled					
	Ceiling (ceiling rose 1860)	**Cornice**	**Wall face**	**Skirting** (replaced after 1860 fire)	**Dado rail** (post 1900)	**Window** (inserted 1965)
Phase 6 1965	cream emulsion on lining paper		cream emulsion	cream gloss paint	cream gloss paint	cream gloss paint
Phase 5 1900	phase 4 retained		grey lead based paint	grey lead based paint	grey lead based paint	
Phase 4 1860 – post fire	ceiling bed ornately painted – ceiling rose added		painted marbling – varnished	painted marbling – varnished		
Phase 3 1832	phase 2 retained		wallpaper (stripped)			
Phase 2 1800	white distemper	phase 1 retained	phase 1 retained			
Phase 1 1760	white distemper	white lead and gilding	lead white tinted with Naples yellow			

Summary of decorative history of the Saloon

The decorative history of the house can now be summarized in a narrative form which is readily understandable by all members of the project team.

Phase 1 – 1760
Room decorated with a partially gilded cornice and yellow wall faces. The decoration of the original dado and skirting cannot be determined as these elements were destroyed in the fire of 1860.

Phase 2 – 1800
The house was sold in 1800 but no significant alterations were carried out in the Saloon apart from the repainting of the ceiling.

Phase 3 – 1832
Accounts held in the family archive indicate that the room was redecorated in 1832 when an expensive Chinese wallpaper was fitted. The gilded decoration on the cornice was retained.

Phase 4 – 1860
Fire of 1860 damaged some of the original skirting and dado and the Chinese wallpaper. The remains of the wallpaper were stripped and an ornate plaster ceiling rose added. The room was then decorated with an ornate painted ceiling and marbled wall faces and skirtings which were recorded in a photograph dated 1900. The original gilding on the cornice was retained.

Phase 5 – post 1900
Sometime after 1900 a dado rail was added. The ornately decorated ceiling and gilded cornice was retained but the wall faces and all of the joinery including the new dado rail was painted grey.

Phase 6   1965
In 1965 the room was used as an office. A new window was inserted in the west wall to provide more light. The ornate ceiling was covered with a lining paper and the walls and the joinery were painted cream. The original gilded decoration of the cornice has been retained.

Once the Architectural Paint Research Chart has been completed the surviving elements may be categorized to determine the significance of the architectural elements and their decorative finishes.

The categorization system for architectural elements and decorative finishes

The APRU has also introduced a post-research categorization system of elements and decorative finishes which assists in highlighting particularly sensitive elements or rare decorative finishes. This system has proved to be a valuable tool for the formulation of conservation and works programmes as well as the future management of the building. This system has been used with success on large-scale projects such as the Little Castle Bolsover and Danson House.

Introduction

This categorization system has been devised for use in buildings which have a varied and complex history and may often contain a wide range of decorative finishes. Establishing specific categories for all of the elements within an interior/building assists the development and implementation of a consistent conservation policy. The categories provide a framework for the informed discussion of conservation and presentation options as well as the future management of the building.

Generally the categorization system is used to highlight original decorative finishes which may be extremely rare and therefore highly significant. It also identifies elements which are perhaps of less significance (i.e. modern additions/repairs). In some buildings later additions may be of greater significance (i.e. alterations by a famous later occupant). Each building will have its own criteria but this can only be defined after the completion of the documentary survey, building analysis and paint research.

If we return to our hypothetical case study of the Saloon we can now consider the options available for the conservation and representation of the room. The detailed investigation of the room has provided valuable information which will inform the decision making process.

Hypothetical case study – the Saloon:
Suggested criteria for assessment of the architectural elements and decorative finishes within the Saloon

Factors to consider:

- The cornice in the room retains its original gilded decorative scheme. This is a rare example of mid-eighteenth-century gilding.
- Structurally the room retains most of the fittings added in 1860 after the fire, the only later additions are the dado rail and window in the west wall.
- It may be possible to reveal the ornately decorated ceiling of 1860 by the removal of the lining paper.
- Technically, the overpaint could be removed from the wall faces and skirting to reveal the 1860 varnished marbled scheme but this may be very costly. The condition of the 1860 scheme would need to be assessed.
- The significance of the insertion of the dado rail and window in the twentieth century requires consideration.

It must be stressed that this is a subjective assessment and Category Types will be refined for each building, and could be altered by any number of factors. In principal, Category A will identify decorative finishes or elements which require special consideration and care, while Categories B, C, D etc. will reflect the relative significance of other finishes/elements.

Category A: Elements which retain original or early decorative finishes which have not been overpainted or otherwise altered. These decorative finishes are very rare.

Category B-1: Elements which bear early decorative finishes which have been overpainted or obliterated. These elements are significant because they bear archaeological evidence of the development of the room.

Category B-2: Elements which bear early decorative finishes which have been overpainted or covered over. These elements are significant because they bear archaeological evidence of the development of the room. It may be possible to reveal specific decorative finishes by the careful removal of later layers. After treatment these elements could then be re-categorized as Category A.

Category C: Elements which could be considered as less significant.

Analysis of paint samples with categorization of elements added to chart

These categories can now be added to the Architectural Paint Research Chart.

At its final stage the chart includes a summary of the key research findings and can be used as a discussion document for future works within the room. The chart should be updated to record any conservation works or redecoration carried out within the room which in the case of the Saloon would be 'Phase 7 Recent Conservation Works and Redecoration 2002'. The final chart should be kept on file and readily accessible for use by house managers. The final version of the chart may be a useful document to present to new project managers or curators as it provides an 'at a glance' record of the location of significant elements

APR Chart 4th stage

Category	Ceiling (ceiling rose 1860)	Cornice	Wall face	Skirting (replaced after 1860 fire)	Dado rail (post 1900)	Window (inserted 1965)
	B-2 (A)	A	B-2 (A)	B-2 (A)	C	C
Main Phases						
Phase 6 1965	cream emulsion on lining paper		cream emulsion	cream gloss paint	cream gloss paint	cream gloss paint
Phase 5 1900	*phase 4 retained*		grey lead based paint	grey lead based paint	grey lead based paint	
Phase 4 1860 – post fire	ceiling bed ornately painted – ceiling rose added		painted marbling – varnished	painted marbling – varnished		
Phase 3 1832	*phase 2 retained*		wallpaper (stripped)			
Phase 2 1800	white distemper	*phase 1 retained*	*phase 1 retained*			
Phase 1 1760	white distemper	white lead and gilding	lead white tinted with Naples yellow			

and provides a simple record of all the alterations which have been carried out within the room.

Using these recording systems it is possible to present complex findings, provide some insight into the decision making process and also record recent conservation works and newly applied decorative schemes.

Appendix II

Paint Strippers: The Naked Truth?

Cathy Proudlove

Paint makers have worked hard over the centuries to produce a tough material which stays put. So it is not surprising that removing paint is not an easy job. Most paint is made up of two basic materials, a pigment (chunks of solid material) and a medium or binder, the stuff which sticks the chunks together. The binder is usually a viscous liquid or gel at the time of application, which then dries to a flexible film. Modern paints are often in emulsion form, which means they can be mixed with water for application. Usually, once that water has dried, the paint will not be readily re-soluble in water, because we wouldn't want paint to wash off too easily as a rule.

Paint binders are nearly always organic materials, their origins are in living things, which includes petrochemicals. This is important when it comes to breaking down the binder to remove the paint, because substances which are effective in re-dissolving tough old paint are likely to be fairly aggressive towards living creatures. Hence, stripping paint can damage your health.

Pigments can be harmful or toxic too, especially lead white, which was the standard white pigment for centuries. Burning paint off with a blow-torch or scraping it off with blades can release pigments into the air where they can be inhaled, and this can be dangerous. For this reason, chemical stripping methods have been preferred for most of the twentieth century.

A passion for painting everything white in the 1960s was soon followed by a more durable obsession with stripped wood, which has only recently abated. Most of this stripping was done with caustic soda, often by the tank-load; a primitive technology. Caustic soda burns the skin, a fact which at least ensured it was treated with some respect by its users. The problem with strippers based on organic solvents is that the harm they can do may not be so immediately obvious.

One such solvent, dichloromethane, was a favourite for the last fifty years, despite its high toxicity and potential as a carcinogen. These disadvantages now require a high level of protection for anyone asked to use this substance. So the race is on to find a safe stripper, and new products are being offered on the market.

A degree of scepticism is in order here. Less familiar chemicals are being used perhaps in the hope that their dangers are not yet recognized. As always, manufacturers love to boast how wholesome their products are while maintaining their commercial advantage through a coy reluctance to specify what is in them. The fact remains that any substance which can break down a coat of paint is likely to be harmful to health. The bigger the job, the bigger the risk. Using a few drops of a substance on an important historic artefact is one thing, applying bucketfuls of the same material to a whole building is quite another. There are other possible methods, which may involve water, steam and mechanical operations, but none of these are appropriate in every case.

Added to its effect on human health, paint stripping often damages the thing underneath far more than the paint itself, which may actually be protective, so careful thought is needed. Paint removal can become an obsession. Is it really necessary?

For the time being at least, a large-scale paint stripping operation should be viewed as a last resort. Quite often existing paint can be left in place, where it may protect earlier decorative layers. These can be identified through cross-sections. Whilst new paint applied over existing layers may not adhere as well, it may still be worth a try. Removing one layer of paint from another, however, is extremely difficult, sometimes impossible in practical terms. So a valued historic finish should never be painted over without first considering reversibility.

Where historic conservation is concerned, the problem may be that an unsuitable paint has been applied which is harming the substrate. The questions should then be asked, just how much damage is the unsuitable paint doing, and is stripping this paint the only realistic solution available? If it is, then the technique used should take into account the nature of the paint, the quantity, the location and the substrate. There will be no single answer, only a 'least worst' solution based on assessment of a wide range of risks.

Bibliography

Association of Local Government Archaeological Officers (ALGAO), *Analysis and Recording for the Conservation and Control of Works to Historic Buildings*, ALGAO, Chelmsford, 1997.

Baty, P., 'The Role of Paint Analysis in the Historic Interior', *Journal of Architectural Conservation*, Vol 1 No1, March 1995, pp. 27–37.

Baty, P., 'To Scrape or Not', *Traditional Paint News*, Vol 1, No 2, October 1996, pp. 4–5.

Belcher, V., Bond, R., Gray, M., and Wittrick, A., *Sutton House. A Tudor Courtier's House in Hackney*, English Heritage and The National Trust Monograph, forthcoming, 2002.

Bristow, I. C., 'Repainting Eighteenth-Century Interiors', *ASCHB Transactions 1982*, Vol VI, 1983, pp. 25–33.

Bristow, I. C., *Architectural Colour in British Interiors 1615–1840*, Yale University Press, New Haven and London, 1996.

Bristow, I. C., *Interior House-painting Colours and Technology 1615–1840*, Yale University Press, New Haven and London, 1996.

Clark, K. (ed.), *Conservation Plans in Action*, English Heritage, London, 1999.

Clark. K., *Informed Conservation*, English Heritage, London, 2001.

Croft-Murray, E., 'Decorative Painting in England 1537–1837', *Country Life*, Vol 1, London, 1962; Vol 2, Feltham, Middlesex, 1970.

Davies, M., 'The Archaeology of Standing Structures', *Australian Journal of Historical Archaeology*, No 5, 1987 pp. 54–64.

Department of National Heritage, *Planning Policy Guidance Note 16: Archaeology and Planning*, HMSO, London, 1990.

Department of the Environment, Transport and the Regions, Department of National Heritage, *Planning Policy Guidance Note 15: Planning and the Historic Environment*, HMSO, London, 1994.

English Heritage, *Dendrochronology: Guidelines on Producing and Interpreting Dendrochronological Dates*, English Heritage, London, 1999.

English Heritage, *Management of Archaeological Projects*, English Heritage, London, 1996.

English Heritage, *Power of the Place: The Future of the Historic Environment*, English Heritage, London 2000.

English Heritage, *Repair Work and Grants from English Heritage: Types of Work Which May Qualify*, English Heritage, London, 1994.

Fowler, J. and Cornforth, J., *English Decoration in the 18th Century*, Barrie & Jenkins, London, 1974.

Harley, R., Artists' Pigments c. 1600–1835: *A Study in English Documentary Sources*, 1970.

Institute of Field Archaeologists (IFA), *Standard and Guidance on the Investigation and Recording of Buildings*, IFA, Manchester, 2000.

Jourdain, M., (pseud. Francis Lenygon), *Decoration in England from 1660 to 1770*, 1914. Jourdain, M., *English Decoration and Furniture of the Later XVIIIth Century (1750–1820)*, 1922.

Kerr, J.S., *The Conservation Plan*, National Trust for New South Wales, Sydney, 2000.

Lea, R., Series of reports on Down House, held at the Historical and Architectural Research Team, English Heritage; Reports commissioned by English Heritage from Keystone Historic Building Consultants on Down House, held at the Historical and Architectural Research Team.

Morris, R., 'Buildings Archaeology', in Wood, J. (ed.), *Buildings Archaeology: Applications in Practice*, Oxbow, Oxford, 1994.

Mynors, C., *Listed Buildings, Conservation Areas and Monuments,* Sweet and Maxwell, London, 1999.

Phillips, M. and Whitney, C., 'The Restoration of Original Paints at Otis House', *Old Time New England,* The Society for the Preservation of New England Antiquities, Vol LXII No 1, summer 1971, pp. 25–28.

Phillips, M., 'Problems in the Restoration and Preservation of Old House Paints', *Preservation and Conservation: Principles and Practices,* The Preservation Press, Washington D.C., 1972, pp. 273–285.

Rodwell, W., *Church Archaeology,* Batsford, London, 1989.

Ruskin, J., 'The Lamp of Memory', *The Seven Books of Architecture,* (1st edition), 1849.

Smith, J., *Art of Painting,* 1676.

Snyder, J.W., Parkes, B.W. and Staehli, A.M., 'Historic Photos as an Aid to Paint Analysis', an unpublished paper presented at the Annual Conference of the Association of Preservation Technology, held in Boston USA, 5–8 October 1988.

Welsh, F., 'Call for Standards', *Association for Preservation Technology Bulletin,* Vol XVIII, No 4, 1986, pp. 4–5.

Index

access to sites 22
   safety and adequacy 24–5
acrylic paints 55
Adam, Robert 12, 42
Adelphi, London 12
Alladyce, Fiona 57
archaeology (archaeologists) 4, 5, 9, 49, 63; see also building analysis
architects 4, 5, 6, 16, 24, 60, 63
architectural elements
   categorization system 70–1
   reinstatement of 39
architectural history 3
Architectural Paint Research Chart 67–71
Architectural Paint Research Unit and Archive, English Heritage 17, 48, 53, 67, 70
archiving 3, 6–7, 49, 50
   of mounted samples 17, 40, 50, 52–3
assessments 13, 15, 49, 68
Audley End, Saloon 14, 52, 55; col. pl. 3.5
Australia, building conservation projects 7

basic competencies, of specialist 50
Battersea Bridge, London 13; col. pls 3.3–3.4
Baty, Patrick ix, 21–5, 53, 58, 60; col. pl. 4.2
Berger, Lewis 9
binders 10, 73
Bolsover Castle (Derbyshire) 27, 56
   Pillar Parlour 15
Boodle's, Saloon 12; col. pl. 2.4
Boyd, Sir John 27
briefing on projects 22–3, 29, 50
Bristow, Ian ix, 9–12, 55, 58, 60–1, 63
Brough, Janet 56, 57
building accounts 13, 24, 68
   technical terms 12
building analysis (buildings' archaeology) 3–4, 5, 6, 14, 16, 29
   costs of 14
building analysts 5, 48, 63, 67
   publication 6
Building at Risk cases 27
building conservation 3, 4–5; see also conservation

Cadw 5
canvas wall linings 31, 32, 33
Carshalton, The Oaks 28
categorization system, for architectural elements and decorative finishes 70–1
ceilings, decorated 37
   health and safety 24
   painted 31, 32, 42
Chambers, Sir William 13
Clark, Kate ix, 3–8, 57–8, 59, 60, 61, 63–4
clients 3, 63
   appropriate information 23
   colour references 25
   as 'doubting Thomas' 24
   English Heritage as 27–30
   experience of researcher known by 16, 22, 50
   feedback system 52
   guidelines 47–8, 50, 51
   health and safety provided by 24–5
   no training for 14
   paint samples archived/owned by 52–3
   private 27, 30, 60
   and reports 17–18
   sharing information 24, 52, 60
   taste of 25, 47–8, 57
   tips on commissioning 21–5
   training for 17
   typical projects 16–17
Colonial Williamsburg (USA) 54
colour
   change of 32
   eighteenth-century 12, 33
   of original scheme 48
   RAL numbers 22
   research on 9–12
colour harmony 24
colour matches 25, 50
colour references 25
commissioning 3, 6, 21–5
   constant consultation 52
   courses for 18
   guidelines (proposed) for 47–50
   if research required 49
   no training for 14

conservation 4–6, 7, 48, 50
conservation officers 6, 37
conservation plan 6, 30, 48, 51
conservation policies 60, 70
conservation/redecoration programme (policy) 49, 50, 52, 53–4
conservators 54
    training in the Netherlands 31–2
contracts 18, 30
Cornforth, John 9
costs 47–8, 50
    of methods of analysis 50
    of samples 22, 57
    of scrapes 58
'cowboys' 22
Croft-Murray, Edward 9
cross-sections (mounted) 10, 12, 21, 58–9, 61, 73
    archived 17; col. pl. 3.6
    cost and number of 22, 57
    funding 57
    Kockengen 33
    National Trust 41, 58
    photomicrograph 10; col. pls 2.2, 3.4, 4.1, 5.3–5.5, 6.5
    reference lists in report 50
    sketch of *11*
curators 18, 24, 52

Danson House 4, 27–30, 58, 59, 60; col. pls 5.1–5.8
Darwin, Charles, Down House 4, 27
databases
    National Trust 42, *43*, 44
    Netherlands 34
Davies, Jane 53, 56–7
decorative finishes *see* finishes
Decorative Historic Interiors Conservation Course, Maastricht 31–2, 59; col. pl. 6.6
definition, of paint research 48
dendrochronology (tree-ring dating) and dendrochronologists 3, 4, 5, 6, 7, 14, 48
dichloromethane 73
distemper 10, 23
documentary research 3, 4, 6, 13, 16, 24, 39, 49, 50, 52, 60, 67–8, 70
Down House 27
Dyrham, Balcony Room 12

Edgar, James ix–x, 37–40, 55, 63
Edwards, John 59
Eltham Palace 27
English Heritage 17, 63
    Architectural Paint Research Archive 53
    Architectural Paint Research Unit 17, 48, 67, 70
    as client 27–30
    conservation programmes 14
    courses for project managers run by 18
    grants from/funding by 5, 6–7
    instructions by 15

    Major Projects Department 27
    overpainting dealt with 56
    publications 6, 54
    risk management 59
    teams 60
    see also guidelines
experience of researcher 16, 21, 22, 50

feedback system 52
fine art conservators 17
finishes (decorative) 13, 24
    categorization system 70
    modern 50
    obliterated 54, 55, 70
    significance of 51, 52
formulation of a policy 49
Fowler, John 9
Friedrichs, Dr Angelique x, 31–4, 52, 54, 59, 63
funding 14, 16–17, 51, 57–8
    application for 5
    for research 49
    for training 18

Garrick, David 12
Gas Chromatography and Mass Spectroscopy (GC-MS) 50
Gibson, David 57
gilding 12, 21, 23, 54
    on Battersea Bridge 13; col. pl. 3.3
gouache 55
Government Historic Buildings Advisory Unit 54
graining 42, 44, 58
grants 6–7, 16, 48, 57; *see also* funding
guidelines, English Heritage (draft) 18, 21, 47–50, 51–4, 63

Ham House 10
Hampton Court, Privy Garden border boards 24
Harley, Rosamond 9
health and safety, paint strippers 73
health and safety issues 24–5; col. pl. 4.2
Heritage Lottery Fund 5, 15, 16, 17, 53
High Performance Liquid Chromatography (HPLC) 50
Hirst, Elizabeth 59–60
historians 59, 60, 67
Historic Buildings Representative (HBR) 41, 42
historic house museums 14, 48
historic paint 9–12, 39, 50
Historic Scotland 5, 18, 57
historical research 42, 47, 48, 53, 59
    Danson House 28
Hodges, David 60
Hoffer, Peter 55, 58
house paint 9, 10, 23
Houthem-St.Gerlach (Netherlands) 32, 33; col. pls 6.1–6.2

Hughes, Helen x, 13–18, 47–50, 52–3, 54–6, 58, 61, 63, 67–71

information
   appropriate 23
   sharing of 24, 52
interim findings 22, 49
interior designers 17
interpretation, of sites 7
Ireland, Richard 55
Islington 37, 57

Jardin, Ian x, 27–30, 59, 60
Jeffrey, Roman 58
Jourdain, Margaret 9

Kedleston, Music Room 10
Kelmash Hall, Northamptonshire 38
Kenwood House 13, *14, 15,* 27, 58
Kew Gardens, Temple of Bellona 13
Knole 59
Kockengen, Utrecht (Netherlands) 32–3; col. pls 6.3–6.4
Köhlen, Johan Josepf 32

Lansdowne House 55
lead paint 23, 33, 55; col. pl. 6.6
Levrant, Stephen 51, 56, 60
Lewis, Pamela 17, 54; col. pl. 3.6
lime plaster 22
linseed oil 23, 33
Listed Building Consent 29, 37–40, 48
   for paint stripping? 15, 37, 38–9, 48, 49, 56
   PPG 15: 5
   required to alter interiors? 37, 38
listed buildings 37, 48, 57
local (planning) authorities 5, 15
   consent for alteration of interiors 38, 39
   conservation officers 37
   paint scheme for interior 57
   paint stripping 38
London, eighteenth-century house 24; col. pl. 4.1

Maastricht, conservation course 31–2, 59; col. pl. 6.6
McDermott, Allyson 54, 55
McLoughlin, David 51, 54, 56
Mansion House, London 10, *11*
marbling 58
material analysis 3, 6, 23, 50
Mears, Roger 51
methodology, reports 17–18
microscopes 10, 12
monitoring bodies, training for 17
mounted cross-sections *see* cross-sections (mounted)
mounted samples *see* paint samples

Naples yellow 33
National Trust 10, 17, 18, 27, 60

cross-sections 41
   formulating procedures for research 41–4
   paint samples 53
   students working with 59
Netherlands 31–4, 63
Nevin, John 56, 57, 59
Nostell Priory 42; col. pl. 8.1

obliterated finishes 54, 55, 70
oil paint 22–3, 56–7
oils 23; *see also* linseed oil
original schemes 12, 14, 16, 28–9, 39, 42, 48, 52, 57
Osborne House 58
Osterley Park 10
overpainting 22, 48, 49, 55, 54, 55, 56, 70, 74
   over stencil 58

painted imitations 23
paint permeability 56
paint research, Danson House 28–9
paint samples 16, 48, 51, 58–9
   archiving of mounted samples 17, 40, 52–3
   chart and categorization 68, 70–1
   costs of 57
   health and safety issues of sampling 24–5; col. pl. 4.2
   location of 17, 42, 53, 58
   mounted 17, 50, 52, 58
   number of 22
   owned by 53
   removal of 50, 51
   in report 50, 52
   sent by post 17, 60–1
paint scrapes *see* scrapes
paint stripping *see* stripping of paint
panelling, painted 31, 32–3
panoramic paintings 32–3
photographs 13, 28, 49, 58, 61, 68
photomicrographs of cross-sections of paint samples col. pls 2.2, 3.4, 4.1, 5.3–5.5, 6.5
pigments 21, 23, 44, 73
   date-relevant 23
   expensive 23
Planning Policy Guidance Note 15: Planning and the Historic Environment (PPG 15) 4–5, 17, 37–40, 63
Planning Policy Guidance Note 16: Archaeology and Planning (PPG 16) 4
planning a programme, guidelines 49–50
plaster, lime 22
polychromatic decoration 22
Port Arthur, Tasmania 3–4, 7
presentation of houses and schemes 7, 16, 27, 28, 42, 70
presentation of interim findings 49
programming, of projects 14, 16–17, 18, 29, 57–8
   and risk management 59–60
project managers 6, 16, 29, 53, 59, 60, 63, 67
   courses for 18

project procedures 50
Proudlove, Cathy x, 56, 73–4
Prussian blue 12, 33
publication 6–7; *see also* reports

railings 23
RAL 22, 25
Rangers House 27
reclamation of obliterated finishes 54
recreation (reconstruction) of historic schemes 14, 48, 49
redecoration 14–15
 documentary references to 4
 National Trust 41, 42, 44
 options available 52
 PPG 15: 38, 39
 programme (policy) 49, 50, 52, 53–4
repairs
 damage from 5
 documented 13
 and planning consent 5
 and samples 22
reports 6–7, 17–18, 22
 appropriate information 23
 in the brief 23
 central archiving of 3
 format of 53
 guidelines 47, 49, 50, 52
researchers (architectural paint)
 basic competencies of 50
 experience of 16, 21, 22, 50
 skills of 23–4, 50
research objectives 49
research plan 50
restoration 3, 5, 28
reversibility 55–6, 74
risk management 59–60
Rosoman, Treve 52, 54

St James' Palace, Queen's Chapel, London 17; col. pl. 3.6
St Paul's, Deptford 58
samples *see* paint samples
sampling strategy 13, 49, 50, 58, 68
scanning electron microscopy 23
Scotland 57
scrapes (paint scrapes) 10, 12, 15, 16, 17, 22, 47, 58–9, 61, 63
 costs 58
 at Kockengen 33
 National Trust 41, 58
 results of 21
Sitwell, Tina xi, 41–4, 53, 58–9
size binders, for paint 10
Smith, John 9, *10*
specification form 42
spectrophotometry 25; col. pl. 4.3

standards 14, 16, 21–2
 guidelines 48
statutory requirements 37–40
stratigraphic interpretation 50
stratigraphy of paint 4, 21, 48, 68
 diagram 17, 54; col. pl. 3.6
stencil patterns 58
stripping of paint 16, 73–4
 differentiated 54
 guidelines 48, 49
 Listed Building Consent needed? 15, 37, 38–9, 56
substrates 10, 56–7, 74
Sutton House 4
Swann, Simon 56
Sydney (Australia), Hyde Park Barracks 7

Taylor, Sir Robert 27, 28
teams, of specialists 6, 14, 29, 30, 42, 59, 60
technical terms 50
 in building accounts 12
thesaurus of terms 44
Thompson, Nicholas 51–2
Tidbury, Roger 58
titanium dioxide 23
training 3, 6, 14, 17, 18, 50, 59, 63
 guidelines 48, 50
Turner, Michael 56
Tynecastle tapestries 54

Uppark, Saloon 12

van Barneveldt, Hendrick 33
verditer 12
Victoria and Albert Museum 10
vinyl emulsions 55

wall linings, painted canvas 31, 32, 33
wall paintings 3, 37
wallpapers 7, 54, 55
wall plaster, cross-section of 10; col. pl. 2.2
Ward, Thomas 42
water-based paints 23, 55, 73
Welsh, Frank 21
West Dean College 18
Westminster, City of 38